AN ANTHOLOGY OF ESSEX

Leez Priory.

AN ANTHOLOGY OF ESSEX

COLLECTED BY ISABEL LUCY AND BEATRICE MARY GOULD

Edited and arranged with additions and a Biographical Index by

CHARLOTTE FELL SMITH

LONDON:
SAMPSON LOW, MARSTON & CO., LTD.

———

1911.

Contents

Foreword

THIS volume owes its being to the enthusiasm of an untiring friend, Mr. H. W. Lewer. His local patriotism demanded nothing less than that Essex should lead the way as pioneer of counties commemorated in the pleasant vogue of the day. She has long been unique in sustaining a county Review, so why not an Anthology?

When the project was first suggested to the Editor it met, I fear, with a reluctant welcome. This attitude, shame be it to say, was even maintained as the topic was renewed at stated intervals ever since. In spite of all deterrents, however, the enthusiast remained serenely firm, and by slow degrees the task began to look not only feasible but strangely alluring. It was at his suggestion that the Misses I. L. and B. M. Gould set to work upon research in the library of their uncle, Mr. I. Chalkley Gould, the well-known Essex antiquary. The books having since his death passed into their possession, these labours were congenial and pleasant, and have been pursued with the most exemplary zeal.

Upon the sound archæological basis thus provided, the Editor has now completed a structure of which only one thing is certain, that it cannot escape criticism. Much of the material at first garnered has had to be eliminated, and many fresh selections have been added—not entirely on the lighter side, although fiction, verse, and recent literature have been widely ransacked. The kindness of friends, both personally known and unknown, in offering the use of original unpublished or privately published matter, I cannot sufficiently acknowledge. Love of our county has been in all cases the common bond. It is a remarkable fact that Essex—the contemned of the hasty stranger—does excite in her own sons and daughters a most enduring instinct of home.

The plan of the work will no doubt meet with disapproval. I shall be told it is far too comprehensive. The net has indeed been spread far and wide. Native writers whom we are proud to call our own ; poets and authors who have cast in their lot with us either temporarily or for good ; poets and novelists around whom our county has thrown its spell (if only during childhood or on a passing visit), each and every one has been welcomed. Nor has it seemed imperative to gather together only passages descriptive of the very inconsonant features of our once-time little kingdom. The result would have been a kind of enraptured guide-book, of which a few jerky pages would have satisfied the most pious Essex lover. Rightly or wrongly, I decided to include in the volume any writers on the county, and county writers on anything. That is to say, on anything edifying or worth preserving. As a consequence, there is great diversity both in style and topics. The reader may flit from the stained-glass conceits of Quarles and Benlowes to the rude human nature, fresh from the soil, of to-day's farm labourer. From Nicholas Breton's or Gabriel Harvey's impassioned love poems to John Clare's lark song to the beans in blossom ; and from Thomas Tusser's rough quiddities to John Davidson's exquisitely perfected lyrics on Epping Forest.

But poetry is not our only fare. This is no boudoir book of pretty ballads. The plaint of hunger and starvation, of untilled lands and undrained marshes, echoes through the pages, as well as the tinkle of sheep bells and the swish of the mowers' scythes. The agues as well as the beauties of the shore and its fleets, claim our notice ; the sad inactivity of the once flourishing smugglers, and the death of many an old feudal custom

A chief aim has been to keep alive something of the

old spirit once dwelling in every 'elm-ringed' farmstead, in the heavy ploughlands of the nine Roding villages, in the light lands of Mid-Essex, and in the silvered saltings and green samphire beds of the coast. To do this seems every whit as important as to vaunt once more and rather boastfully, our glorious Tudor architecture and our many famous 'worthies.' Of the former we have a pictorial example in Mr. J. Charles Wall's Frontispiece of the tower of Lord Rich's splendid gateway, as it appears after restoration by its present owner, Mr. Hughes-Hughes. To the last, full justice could not possibly be done in a work of this kind. A very few of the great company of our notable men and women have been named : the purely literary men of the county in the past receive perhaps scantier notice in these pages than any other product. Even the greed of that licensed pilferer, the anthologist, has stopped short of assimilating fragments from John Gower, Thomas Langford, or Thomas Netter ; Dr. William Gilbert or Jeremy Bentham ; not to mention reverend divines like Bishop Hall, the puritan John Owen, the royalist Gauden, the historian Merivale, the great legal writer Comyns, or the translator 'Hesiod' Cooke. Similarly, pages of rare feats, customs, folk-tales, quaint curiosities, and interesting localities must remain unquoted and unsung. Of the muse of the sententious Quarles, perhaps some will be tempted to say there is more than enough, although few will deny the sound ethics of his prim couplets. To all the unnamed writers who have celebrated our county in prose or verse and whose names from one cause or another are absent here, we tender a regretful apology.

Of the material collected by the diligence of the compilers much has had to be rejected as unsuited to our purpose, though all of it was interesting. The chief virtue of a county anthologist lies, it seems, more in omission than in appropriation. And our county is practically inexhaustible. The sharp contrasts it presents are scarcely equalled in kind by any other.

Compare the rolling stretches of high lowland around the villages of Henham, Widdington, and Chrishall in the North West—think of them as red with clover, yellow with mustard seed in blossom, or in emerald of peafields (as they may be seen in the background of a Clausen idyll)—with the dreary lines of brick boxes radiating from the Moloch Suburbia. Contrast East Ham and Barking, or even Dagenham and Corringham, with lonely Foulness or St. Peter's-on-the-wall. The onsweeping tide of London has crept up to the very rim of our virgin Forest. It is spreading farther and farther around our principal towns. Even in that district where a good twenty-five miles lies between railway and railway, prosperity, haste, and good farming are changing the lovely aspect of twenty-five years ago. Timber trees in the hedge rows are being ruthlessly felled. Hedges are trimmed till they almost resemble a hog's mane. The wild guelder rose, the coral berried spindle-wood, the purple dogwood, to say nothing of the sweet wild rose, have a hard struggle for existence on these farms. Again, there is the wild beauty of those bird-haunted creeks of our sharply indented coast. The tide-swept shores of our five estuaries of Stour, Colne, Blackwater, Crouch and Thames, where ooze and firm mud end in grey saltings and green pastures, offer features hard to match. Danbury, Woodham Walter and Galleywood Commons, Tiptree Heath, and Kelvedon Common near Brentwood, provide great stretches of open country where heather, gorse, bracken and birds are the sole denizens. The chalk hills of Bartlow and Saffron Walden give us an entirely different aspect and flora; Constable's Vale of Dedham is fixed for ever as the type of rural beauty.

Something of each and all will be found in the succeeding pages. Something of our great affection for the soil from which we sprang has been put into words for us by such writers as Mr. Reginald Beckett and Miss Burmester, such poets as Mr. Cripps and Mr. Cranmer Byng. If the reader—alien born—should consider the note of eulogy has been too uniformly struck, that at least is not the fault either of our county, or of its people. We are surely altruistic enough to wish that others may come and learn our pastoral beauties by heart for themselves. For not all our most enthusiastic authors are natives of Essex. And there are living writers who have embedded the very spirit of our natives and of our marsh villages in their stories, and yet they must remain unrepresented here, by reason of the difficulty of extraction.

If a few of our authors prove little known to the general reader, some extremely familiar favourites will be found among the poems. It was impossible to omit Ann Taylor's beautiful appeal to the best influences of childhood, or the hardly less-known stanzas from *In Memoriam*, inspired by the Waltham Abbey chime of bells. William Morris's intense love of beauty was based upon nature, and it is our pride to remember that Essex was his birthplace and the inspirer of his earliest ideals. It is not to be expected that standards such as these could be maintained throughout a work of this kind. The range of a county anthology is necessarily contracted, and it cannot aspire to be of the highest, or even a consistent literary value. The literary rendering of cogent and essential facts or features, in themselves desirable, is often far to seek. It is incredible how many dreary volumes of verse and description even a county like ours can suggest! The compilers have waded through book after book without finding a single gleam of inspiration. If the Editor has suffered some things to pass that seem mere padding, she may hope that the intrinsic value of the greater part included, will help to redeem the palpable literary shortcomings of the rest.

It is perhaps not too much to hope that one result of our labours will be to stimulate those who do not possess the volumes from which we have culled, to turn to them, while it is obvious that in our modest anthology, those who acquire it will own a library in microcosm, and in the most portable form.

I must here express grateful thanks to the Rev. A. S. Cripps, Mr. Lancelot Cranmer-Byng, Miss Olive Venner, and Mr. W. H. Harwood for having contributed original verse to this volume. From the two first I have also received many helpful suggestions. Miss Frances Waldegrave Meadows has given to the Misses Gould the use of a poem by her father, a former vicar of Chigwell. Mr. George Courtauld kindly allows me to quote verses which he has privately printed.

The authors next named permit quotation from their copyright works ; they and their publishers deserve especial gratitude :—Miss Frances C. Burmester, Mr. Thomas Barrett Lennard, Mr. Reginald Beckett, Mr. Arthur H. Byng, Mr. Lancelot and Mr. Hugh Cranmer-Byng, Mr. S. L. Bensusan, Mr. R. Y. Bevan, Mr. W. Gurney Benham and Mr. Charles E. Benham, whose Essex Ballads have been freely offered, Mr. Edward North Buxton, Mrs. Chaplin, Mr. Miller Christy, Mr. S. A. Courtauld, Mrs. John Davidson and Mr. Grant Richards (for a short poem and a portion of a longer one on Epping Forest, by John Davidson), Mr. Edward A. Fitch, Miss E. Fox Howard, Mr. H. Lewis Jones, Mr. H. Rider Haggard, Colonel Lockwood, Mr. Arthur Morrison (for kind interest in the Anthology as well as delightful prose), the Rev. Severne Ashhurst Majendie, Mr. J. E. Patterson, Mr. J. W. Robertson-Scott, and Mr. J. Horace Round for permission to quote a passage from his work on the great Earl of Essex (Longmans).

The Trustees of William Morris have most kindly allowed numerous quotations from the inexhaustible well of his writings.

The Editors of the *Spectator*, the *Nineteenth Century*, *National Review* and *Cornhill Magazine* have been good enough to sanction the use of material that has appeared in their pages. Some verses issued in the *Epping Gazette Series* appear by the proprietor's permission. By consent of the Essex Archæological Society a quotation is made from the *Transactions*. From the *Essex Review* many contributions have been levied, and my thanks are once more due to all those who help to carry it on.

If any name is inadvertently omitted here and passages have been included without due acknowledgment, I trust this apology for it will be accepted.

The courtesy and generosity of the undermentioned publishers must be sincerely recorded :—

Messrs. A. and C. Black for quotations from Moncrieff's *Essex*.

Mr. B. H. Blackwell, of Oxford, for a poem in Cripps' *Lyra Evangelistica*.

Messrs. Blackwood & Co. for an extract from Anthony Trollope's *Autobiography*.

Mr. A. H. Bullen for a few lines from Barrett's *Essex: Highways, Byways and Waterways*.

Messrs. Chatto & Windus for quotations from Besant's *All in a Garden Fair*, and Tompkins' *Marsh Country Rambles*.

Messrs. Constable & Co. for short passages from the *Victoria History of Essex*, vol. ii., and *The Houblon Family*, by Lady Alice Archer Houblon.

Messrs. J. M. Dent & Sons for valuable portions of Beckett's *Romantic Essex* (the verses on p. 2 are his own) ; as well as others from Perceval's *London's Forest*.

Mr. Fisher Unwin and Mr. A. H. Byng for an anecdote from *The Autobiography of an English Gamekeeper*.

Mr. Henry Frowde, The Oxford University Press, for verses from Dean Carrington's *Anthology of French Poetry* ; and the Clarendon Press, Oxford, for a paragraph from Weston's *School History of Essex*.

Mr. Heinemann for leave to cite 'The Song of the Spade' from Patterson's *Tillers of the Soil*, and for delightful passages from Bensusan's *Country Side Chronicle*.

Messrs. Longmans, Green & Co. kindly arranged for the excerpts from William Morris's *Earthly Paradise*, *News from Nowhere*, *Dream of John Ball*, *The Wood beyond the World*, and *Under an Elm Tree*.

Mackail's *Life of Morris* and Haggard's *Rural England* are also quoted with their consent, as is my own *Mary Rich.*

Messrs. Macmillan give permission to reprint Locker Lampson's charming poem on 'The Broad Oak of Hatfield Forest,' from *London Lyrics;* also to quote from Atkinson's *Forty Years in a Moorland Parish*; from Dutt's *Highways and Byways in East Anglia*, and the short passage from Tennyson's *Life.*

Messrs. Marshall Brothers permit citations from Spurgeon's *Autobiography* and his other works.

Messrs. Methuen have generously allowed extracts to be made from Sir Evelyn Wood's *From Midshipman to Field Marshal*, Dr. J. C. Cox's *Essex*, and Arthur Morrison's works.

Messrs. Mills and Boon are to be thanked for a quotation from Sir Claude de Crespigny's *Forty years of a Sportsman's Life.*

Mr. John Murray heartily accorded the use of paragraphs from Borrow's *Romano Lavo-Lil*; and from Thorne's *Handbook to the Environs of London;* as well as 'The Danbury Swallow,' verses written by the late Duke of Argyll.

Sir Isaac Pitman and Sons grant leave to take a short excerpt from Canon Vaughan's *Lighter Studies of a Country Rector.* I regret inability to quote from his delightful sketch of John Ray.

Mr. Edward Stanford is the publisher of Buxton's *Guide to Epping Forest*, from which we are enabled to take a short quotation.

Messrs. Smith, Elder & Co., kindly allow the insertion of incomparable descriptions of the marshes from that Essex classic, Baring-Gould's *Mehalah.* Margaret Veley's *Marriage of Shadows and other Poems* is also their publication.

Messrs. Ward, Lock & Co. give leave for two extracts from Kernahan's *Captain Shannon* to appear.

April, 1911. C. F. S.

LOVE FOR OUR COUNTY
AND
ITS FAMILIAR FEATURES

B

'I come not from Heaven, but from Essex.'

WILLIAM MORRIS, *Dream of John Ball.*

'Where peasants tending upland kine
Scan distant sails, and scent the brine.'

'By night and day, their marshy verge
The creeks uncover and submerge,
And draw into their arms the streams
That thread the country of our dreams.'

'From Langdon's shoulder the glad beholder
Gains sweeps yet bolder o'er hill and lea,
Where, widening ever in long endeavour,
The glistening river o'ertakes the sea.'

'There, morn to eve, the sunlight falls,
On shingled spires, on gable walls,
On sloping pastures, wheatfields wide,
And woods where shy wild creatures hide.'

REGINALD A. BECKETT, *Romantic Essex.*

Essex

Love for our County

I GO through the fields of blue water
On the south road of the sea:
High to north, the East country
Holds her green fields to me,
For she that I gave over
Gives not over me.

Last night I lay at Good Easter
Under a hedge I knew;
Last night in wood by High Easter
I trod the May-floors blue:
Out of the sea the sun came
Bidding me wake and rue.

Roding, that names eight churches
(Banks with the paigles pight),
Chelmer, whose mill and willows
Keep one red tower in sight,
Under the Southern Cross run
Beside our ship to-night.

Ah! I may not go back now,
Neither be turned nor stayed,
Yet should I live, I'd seek her,
Once that my vows are paid,
And should I die, I'd haunt her,
I being what God made.

England has greater counties,
Their peace to hers is small.
Low hills, rich fields, calm rivers!
In Essex, seek them all—
Essex, where I that found them
Did but lose them all!

ARTHUR SHEARLEY CRIPPS (*s.s. Goorkha, May* 1906.)

Love for our County

AND now I come to John and Alice Lott. I have kept them to the last because I love them so much, and not only do I love them, but I love the Essex Hundred in which they lived, and I want to go back again, in memory, and stand in the midst of its great flat fields, in which the ploughs will be busy during this month of November, and look across the brown marshes towards the sea until I can almost fancy that I hear the roll of the waves and feel the salt air biting my cheek! Perhaps I love it better in memory than I do in fact. I go there but seldom now, and then its keen breezes pierce me through and through; but I know that, though I am a wanderer in many countries—one of earth's tramps—yet still, amidst old German towns, with all their grotesque charm; amongst the olive-gardens and orange-groves of Southern France; on the shores of the Mediterranean, where Nature puts forth her most glowing colours, her greens, her reds, and her blues, preening herself as it were, parraquet-like in the sunlight; or if I dwell in picturesque mediæval Flanders; beyond all, in fair Italy, that spiritual land in which the soul seems to rise above the body—even in Florence, the city of flowers where—

'The lazuline ether ascends and swells;'

yes, even there, amidst all its wealth of art and lavishness of beauty, I return in heart to Essex! There are mists of tears through which I look at it with the eyes of my spirit; but we love the things we weep over better than those we laugh for; and so I take my pleasure sadly, and stray once more along the dull roads with the straight, treeless hedgerows on either side; I pass the Church set away at the far end of a big field, the churchyard full of the dead of bygone generations. I go through the village street, I look lingeringly over the wall into the garden where I played as a child, up and down the straight gravel walks, between flower beds edged with prim box plants; I cross the marshes, and reach at length the shore where John and Field picked up the liquor; I gaze at Mussel Island and think of the great storm and Jake's path of glory!

FRANCES G. BURMESTER, *John Lott's Alice*, 1902.

IF in this I can dedicate a thankful heart to the great and almighty disposer of all things, it shall be His, because He made it, he mov'd it. Every morning begins a mercie to us; every night concludes one: so the morning and the evening are the day of mercie. But theise, being common, take no great impression in us. If wee cou'd sift out the grossnes of our owne corruptions, wee should find a pure and most refined power working for us, and striving with us.

And it is not the least of the blessings that I have cause to bee thankfull for, that God hath provided for mee (now that almost all the whole kingdom is in a miserable and devastated condition) a beeing in Essex; where by the sence of charitie more than suffring, wee participate of the publique affliction.

ARTHUR WILSON, *Autobiography* (1649).

FIELDS of dear Essex, if estranged from thee,
By mountains, lakes, or distant breezy sea,
The mind untravell'd still full oft repairs,
To ascertain how each kind neighbour fares;
And when the days appointed cheering come,
Those days are doubly blessed when welcom'd home.

P., *Essex Literary Journal*, 1839.

The Soul of Essex

Love for our County

THE reader must have perceived that with me Essex is a passion—almost a religion. Sometimes in the London streets, especially during long summer days, the thought comes over me of churches, inns, or clustered villages that I know, how they stand quietly through the hours, the sunlight travels round them and fades, and all the time perhaps there is no one there who appreciates their beauty as I do—at least, I am not there. This thought brings a strange mixture of exaltation and despondency. When my desire is fulfilled and I am bodily amidst the scenes I love, all else seems vain. I feel that I have come home; and I ask myself why have I been away so long? So much time seems to have been wasted. The curious thing is, that there is no disillusion; everything seems more beautiful than I remembered or imagined it.

REGINALD A. BECKETT, *Romantic Essex*, 1901.

My World

O LITTLE fields hemmed in and furtive lanes
And shy, green worlds by circling oaks embrowned,
I love you! how I love you! when the bound
Frost-twinkling furrows revel in their chains;
When slender blades are drawn from sheathing grains;
When drifting apple blossoms stain the ground;
When, in the night, swells and recedes around
The overwhelming sadness of the rains.

Within your midst, O little realm, I set
My rose of life, the shrine to which I kneel:
Ah! guard her well for she was made to feel

Our passing glooms, our rapture and regret ;
The song that eddies down the mornlands wet,
And the rare notes that faltering dusks reveal.

L. CRANMER-BYNG, *An English Rose, &c.*, 1906.

At Michaelmas

Harvest Thanksgiving Day in an Essex Village.

ARE all those fallen Angels fall'n so far
That none regrets his star?
Is there to-day no would-be Reaper blithe,
With heavenly hook and scythe—
Who cries 'Alas! I reap but house-top grass'?
Love-in-the-Ruins, unto Thee I pray
For exiles all to-day!

This very day—where Essex stubbles shine—
On one small happy shrine,
The shingled spire with mellow mirth will call,
From street and farm and hall,
Folk unto priest—for reaper's Lauds and Feast ;
What time my county sings her carrying song—
Christ, is it sin to long?

ARTHUR SHEARLEY CRIPPS, *Lyra Evangelistica*, 1909.

Ongar : A Reverie

OH quaint old Essex town! your sheltered ways
Have fared so gently in this vale of tears ;
That looking back with thought of other days,
One sees no change to mark the passing years.
I hear the same wind whisp'ring thro' the trees,
Where Livingstone once wandered with his books :
I hear the same low murmur of the bees,
And recognise the cawing of the rooks.

Oh, peaceful Essex town! you're very old;
The Romans built within your lines a camp;
Your stones have oft resounded, so I'm told,
With Cæsar's sturdy warriors' martial tramp:
I hear their shouts re-echo in the breeze;
Ye Britons, read about them in your books;
The sounds of Roman axe and falling trees
Are heard above the cawing of the rooks.

Oh, quiet old Ongar town! I've heard it said
When Cromwell and his Ironsides held their sway,
That many of your sons both fought and bled
To help the King they loved to win the day.
I heard the cry 'For Cromwell and the Lord!'
Whilst students donned the helm and closed their books,
The sound of war's alarms, the clash of pike and sword
Were heard above the cawing of the rooks.

Some day, I hope my ship will come to town,
And bring to me the fortune overdue;
I'll buy a little cot and settle down,
And make my home, old Ongar town, with you.
I'll rise each day to greet the early dawn,
And dawdle with my fishing and my books;
I'll wander through the cornfields in the morn,
And listen to the cawing of the rooks.

A.L.M. *Loughton Gazette*, April 1910.

To Thaxted Spire

MAJESTIC giant! lordly Spire!
What joys thy aspect doth inspire,
When absent long from home and thee,
Thy towering beacon first I see!

Thy glittering vane (seen many a mile),
Proclaims my welcome with a smile ;
And tells of home and evening fire,
Not far from thee, dear Thaxted Spire !

On Sabbath morn thou greet'st mine eyes,
I see thee 'pointing to the skies !'
And thoughts of heaven my breast inspire,
Aided by thee, thou sacred Spire !

What lovely views of fairyland
Thy lofty summit can command ;
All that a poet could desire,
Meets thy far ken, proud Thaxted Spire !

And I would wish, whene'er I die,
Beneath thy shade in peace to lie,
And greet, when human joys expire
Thine hallow'd precincts—Thaxted Spire !

J. T., *Essex Literary Journal.*

Home's Best

TRAVELLING folk in search of the picturesque very often go a great number of miles to see places not nearly so interesting, after all, as their own. But to many a change is the pleasure of life. In our day-dreams of contemplative felicity, when we have looked at the clouds traversing the lovely heavens, we have thought insensibly of spots over which those self-same clouds might, in their rapid careerings, quickly dispose themselves, with peculiar delight—a delight, however, which, from various causes, may never more be excited, in our minds, by like scenes and similar treatment. To give indulgence still to the observant faculties we are thus led to think more and more of domestic haunts and local beauties. Yet this is no new indulgence; for often after long protracted wanderings, and many recordings with diurnal fullness, we have come back to Essex and to home, feeling most deeply satisfied that, notwithstanding we had enjoyed many pleasing varieties of hill, dale, and woodland, those of our own place and neighbourhood were clearly entitled to our warmest and most affectionate admiration.

JOHN PLAYER,
Sketches of Saffron Walden and Vicinity, 1845.

Praise of Essex

THIS shire is moste fatt, frutefull, and full of profitable thinges, exceeding (as farr as I can finde) anie other shire, for the generall comodeties, and the plentie. . . . This shire seemeth to me to deserve the title of the Englishe Goshen, the fattest of the Lande: comparable to Palestina, that flowed with milke and hunnye. But I can not comende the healthfulness of it: and especiallie nere the sea coastes, Rochford, Denge, Tendering hundredes, and other lowe places about the creekes, which gave me a moste cruell quarterne fever. But the manie and sweete comodeties countervayle the daunger. . . . It is full of parkes. This shire is well planted with noblemen and gentlemen, as also not a few sufficient and able yeomen.

JOHN NORDEN, *Description of Essex*, 1594.

ESSEX is a country of great breadth, very fruitful, abounding in saffron, very well stored with wood, and exceeding rich. *Its familiar Features*

WILLIAM CAMDEN, *Britannia*, 1586.

A FAIR County, bearing the full proportion of five and thirty miles square, plentifully affording all things necessary to man's subsistance, save that the *Eastern part* is not very healthfull or the Aire thereof.

THOMAS FULLER, *Worthies of England*, 1662.

THE County of Essex is one of the best situated in this kingdom, on account of its nearness to the capital, conveniency of water-carriage, good roads in general, and other great advantages. This county is not filled with light sands, apt to be blown about with every high wind ; nor is it covered with barren rocks, or dreary mountains ; but the surface of it is, in general, level. However, it is not a dead flat, but diversified with agreeable eminences and fruitful dales ; the latter watered, in general, with brooks, or rills of water. . . . The country being inclosed makes it much more comfortable to live and travel in, than such as is quite open and exposed, without the least shelter, to all the inclemencies of wind and weather : and it also makes every man's property, whether great or little, much securer, and more his own, than when it is unfenced, and liable to the encroachments of every joint commoner, or greedy neighbour. To which add, that the trees in the fences afford a great quantity of fuel, a matter of no small importance. The soil is various, but in general, good. Very little there is but that is profitable, more or less.

PHILIP MORANT, *History of Essex*, 1760-8.

How little known

Its familiar Features

HERE is a beautiful district lying at our very doors, which to the great majority of travellers from the metropolis is a veritable unknown land. Yet the historic interest, at least, of a county situated so near to London and the Thames, and necessarily the theatre of many events that have helped to shape our destinies, must be obvious enough. . . . It is an article of faith with many that there are no hills in Essex. With those who know better this assertion only provokes a smile; but, as happens with most vulgar errors, it dies hard. It is true that other parts of England can show bolder heights, lovelier rivers, more opulent architecture than Essex; but for variety of interest, and for a certain homelike sweetness which excites not only admiration but affection, Essex bears the palm.

REGINALD A. BECKETT, *Romantic Essex.*

PERHAPS, of all the counties of England, the one of which the least is known by English people generally is the county of Essex. It has been given a bad name as a flat county, an uninteresting county, an aguish county, a county without society, a hopelessly unresidential county; in fact, so many bad names have been bestowed upon it that it has been hanged over and over again, and may be reckoned as a dead county. Yet there is a great deal of life actually remaining in Essex, and life, too, which is not without its attractiveness for those who will take the trouble to study it. . . . If you want to see the country at its best you must go down into it in July. Then these great fields are one waving expanse of corn, standing strong and yellow, waiting for the reaping machines to come and destroy their beauty. The soil is of good quality, and though farmers are a race that grumbles, the crops are plentiful, and the grain some of the best that goes into the market.

Its familiar Features

FRANCES G. BURMESTER, *John Lott's Alice.*

THOSE who know not Essex, or those who have simply scoured through it by express on the way to some seaside resort, or have raised noisome clouds of dust along its main roads in their equally rapid motor cars, can have but little conception of the numerous charming vignettes of local scenery which abound in the less frequented parts of the interior and of the coast-line, or by the riverside of this great and varied county. J. C. COX, *Essex* (Little Guides), 1909.

ESSEX has some cause to complain of being neglected by strangers who are apt to turn away from its river flats and sea edges. But behind that unalluring rim the ground rises in undulating uplands of often pleasant and sometimes lovely scenery; indeed it has been maintained that the finest bits of sylvan scenery within reach of London belong to this homely county, cut off from the regard of the West-End by miles of monotonously mean streets. It may at least claim a general aspect of characteristic English rurality, nor need any county be too modest as to charms which have been celebrated by such an artist as Constable; where Dickens, Besant, and other novelists have laid their schemes; where poets like William Morris and Coventry Patmore got their youthful impressions of nature. Even from the railway one can often see how this is a land of homely pleasantness, of unobtrusive charms, of half-hidden allurements, that to sympathetic tastes take no mean rank in the scale of beauty.

A. R. HOPE MONCRIEFF, *Essex*, 1909.

Its familiar Features

CHURCHES and houses alike were built with the materials which were ready to hand. There is much timber in the building, because Essex has few quarries. In hundreds of churches, too, you may see the relics of the Roman occupation. The Roman bricks are worked into the lower parts of the walls; flint commonly comes above the brick, and stout timbers are used not only for the roof but in the whole construction. Sometimes the spire is made entirely of wood, and we agree with Mr. Beckett that there is something beautiful and touching in the exaltation to this use of the characteristic material of the county. We might add to what he says that no wood was used so often in building as chestnut. When a beam was wanted for a house, or a roof for a church, chestnut was the wood, no doubt because of the belief that no insect takes kindly to it. The great building age of what is now rural Essex must have come immediately after the suppression of the monasteries, and you can hardly go into an Essex village without finding a Tudor house.

If it be a manor-house, it may have a moat, or an old monkish fish-pond, and perhaps the pigeon tower, which dates from the times when the lord of the manor had his rights of pigeonry, is still standing. The old inns have a spaciousness which informs you of the well-being of agricultural Essex when they were built. Where the land is good there the inns are good also; where the land is poor the inns are built on niggard lines. If, as has been said, there are no great buildings in Essex, there is still no town in England with so perfect a Roman wall as that at Colchester. . . . Roman, Norman, and Dane, can be traced very easily by the names they have left in Essex even where they cannot be traced by their fortifications. The names are extraordinarily attractive. Consider the Saxon Guestingthorpe, the Norman Layer-de-la-Haye or Tolleshunt d'Arcy, the Danish Thorpe-le-Soken, and then such odd names as Wendens Ambo and Shellow Bowells.

Its familiar Features

As an example of the out-of-the-worldness of some Essex villages take the piece of country, about twelve miles long, between Ongar and Dunmow. Here are three groups of villages known as the Rodings, the Lavers, and the Easters. It is a cornland traversed by grassy lanes and no railway near it. Every village has its windmill near the church. You can walk through the lanes for miles without seeing a human being. . . . No, Essex is not dull, nor flat, nor ugly; it has a mellow sweetness of its own, a quaint diversity, and a scarcely injured aspect of antiquity, as Constable and William Morris very well knew.

The Spectator, 28th Sept. 1907.

Wooded Essex

ON entering Essex the road is more than pleasant. It leads through woody lanes which grow more beautiful as we approach Colchester. Ardley-woods, which in a manner surrounded us, afforded everywhere the most pleasing sylvan scenes—sometimes retiring to a distance, sometimes advancing, now incircling a common with its cottages, and forming a background behind them, then closing up the whole road so as to leave the eye at a loss where it could break out. Nor were these effects produced by copse-wood, or paltry trees, but by noble oaks and elms, many of which, even single, had dignity enough to grace a scene.

WILLIAM GILPIN, *Tour in Essex* (1769).

Fine Timber

Its familiar Features

OF all the elms that ever I saw, those in the south side of Dovercourt, in Essex, neere Harwich, are the most notable, for they grow (I meane) in crooked maner, that they are almost apt for nothing else but navie timber, great ordinance and beetels; and such thereto is their naturall qualitie, that being used in the said behalfe, they continue longer, and more long than anie the like trees in whatsoever parcell else of this land, without cuphar, shaking or cleaving, as I find.

WILLIAM HARRISON, *Description of England*, 1587.

Landmarks

JAMES ALTHAM (Mark Hall, Latton) to Sir W. Masham at Oates (1637), as to felling trees on Thornwood Common, which, he says: 'As you were informed, were annoyance to the road. They were anciently set there as marks to distinguish the parishes of Latton and Weald, and, as I am able to prove, have been so reputed to be for above sixty years, till of late years the inhabitants of Weald, for what advantage I know not, desiring to alter the bounds of their parish, have cut them up (as they pretend at your command), and placed another, and made a way there where never was any before, which being a great prejudice to my inheritance, I pulled up, with an intent to place trees there, to supply the offices of those which were taken away. For this we are presented at the Quarter Sessions . . . I crave that Weald men may mend their own ways and not encroach upon my inheritance.'

Essex Review, 1908.

Churchyard Trees

THE elm and the yew tree are in thought most frequently associated with church-yards, and in certain parts of England they are undoubtedly the commonest churchyard trees. . . . In Essex especially, the land of elm trees, many an interesting church is guarded by ancient elms, in the hollows of which the jackdaws build their nests, and from which the moping owl issues at eventide for its silent flight over the glebe. The stately church of Finchingfield, associated with memories of Stephen Marshall, the famous Puritan preacher in the days of the Commonwealth, is sheltered by some magnificent elms, which may have witnessed the changes of that stirring time. In the same neighbourhood, the peaceful churchyard of Black Notley is separated from the adjoining cornfields by a long line of ancient elms, which stand sentry over the pyramidal tomb erected to the memory of our illustrious naturalist, John Ray.

Its familiar Features

JOHN VAUGHAN,
Lighter Studies of a Country Rector, 1909.

Birds of the Shore

THE seaboard of Essex, with its extensive 'saltings' covered only occasionally by the highest tide, its considerable mud-flats, left regularly uncovered at low water, and the grass-covered marshes definitely recovered from the sea, form favourable feeding grounds and breeding haunts for both waders and web-footed birds. Wildfowl are still numerous, though a mere fraction of the myriads which formerly abounded. The sites of thirty-five old decoys

Its familiar Features have been identified. Of these only two are now regularly worked, namely, those of the Grange and Marsh House, both in Tillingham parish. The Brent goose formerly appeared off this coast in almost fabulous numbers, and it is still numerous in severe weather. There are four heronries in the county, namely: Birch Hall, about 200 nests; Wanstead Park, the property of the Corporation of London, some 50 nests on tall elms; St. Osyth's Priory, from 30 to 40 nests in two small colonies; and Boreham House, about 25 nests. The raven, alas! is now only a rare autumn or winter visitor. Early in last century it was fairly common throughout the county, but has gradually dwindled. Up to 1890 it continued to breed regularly in very small quantities among the highlands and lowlands on the coast. The magpie is almost extinct, though the jay remains fairly common. The only gull which breeds in the county, and that in small and diminishing numbers, is the black-headed gull, known locally as the peewit gull. The starling, in Essex as elsewhere, is rapidly increasing; its bold, piratical ways are hurtful to several other species, particularly to the rapidly diminishing woodpecker, which it frequently ejects from its breeding holes.

J. C. Cox, *Essex* (Little Guides).

The Smuggler's Paradise

EXAMINE a large map of Essex and you will see how truly the county was 'made a purpose for smugglers.' Run your eye along the marvellously contorted coast-line from Shoeburyness to St. Osyth Point. There are at least fifty well-defined rivers or creeks or outfalls; to search the coast for some notorious gang on a dark night was to look for the proverbial needle in a haystack. And westwards, from Shoebury-ness to Tilbury, the riverside was almost as convenient for this traffic. Many inns are said to bear the same name which they bore when smugglers haunted their parlours, and when smuggled spirits lay below in artfully contrived 'hides.' What the artificial deep ways, cut on the slope of hills near the sea, were to the Cornishmen, the sea wall was to the man of Essex. Both afforded excellent shelter when goods—whether kegs, bales, or what not—were being stealthily conveyed up-country. In the parish of Tollesbury alone there are perhaps fifteen miles of sea-wall, much of which dates back to the times when the industrious Dutchman gained both pudding and praise by his skill in rearing earthworks to resist the encroachments of the sea. The preventive officer could see nothing unless actually upon the wall, in which case, if there was light enough to serve his purpose, it also served to render him a conspicuous mark for a bullet. A revenue cutter, pursuing a small smuggling craft along one of the winding creeks in the neighbourhood of the Blackwater, could see nothing of what was going forward on land, where even the country gentleman was in league with the smugglers, often sending ponies to the appointed landing-place to bear the kegs post-haste many miles inland.

Its familiar Features

HERBERT W. TOMPKINS,
Marsh Country Rambles, 1904.

'SMUGGLERS,' said Father William, 'th' Lord love an' keep ye! I knows a might about they. Do ye plenish me fire an' draw th' curtain, an' I'll tell ye 'bout 'em. . . . When I were a boy, th' river were full on 'em. Come across

Its familiar Features

th' water from 'Olland, what's out that way, I'm told. Come wi' rum, an' gin, an' bacca, an' lace, same 's what wimmen wear in Lunnon. Lord! I weren't on th' marsh wi' me sheepses f'r nothin'. There's many things I seed, bein' very 'eedful. . . . It's many a cargo I've seed run up the river; an' when I were a young man, 'twerent 'Cisemen nor Reveny cutters, neither, what could stop they. The boats used to come up wi' the toide, an' drop th' stuff wi' floats an 'sinkers, an' then out they'd goo agen; an' if chance toimes they met a Reveny cutter, they was jest 'ard-workin' fisher-folk what 'adn't never done no 'arm to nobody. An' then th' little boats 'd put out' o ere an' bring th' stuff ashore, an' bury some on it, an' take the rest inland, wery slow like an' careful. Lord! I've knowed th' 'Cisemen to come a-gallopin' down th' road, an' a score o' bar'ls under th' hedge right in sight, if it 'adn't bin so dark, th' fools! . . . Love ye, I'm some sorry they've all went. . . . They've broke it up wi' coast-guardses, an p'licemen what lives on th' river, an' 'spectors, an' sich like. An' th' men what did ut is dead, an' they schools ha' spoilt th' young 'uns. A man don't belong to hisself no more, an' th' business is gone, like them what did ut. Them what should ha' bin runnin 'bacca an' gin like ther fathers afore 'em, an' bringin somethin' chance times to a pore ole man what give ther fathers good adwice, they're jest fishin' f'r dabs, or shooting on t' sea-wall, or down at th' Wheat-shiff, drinkin stuff what ain't 'arf so good, an' costs 'em 'most fower toimes as much. An' I ain't no patience wi' they. An' I don't take n' count o' fish, an' never did, an' they buds is some 'ard to pluck, for me fingers is wery stiff, an' I keeps all on a breakin' o' th' skin. But I've me ole corkscrew, an' do ye look at ut starin' at ye fr' th' wall, an' no wark f'r th' pore thing to do these days. There's toimes when I goos out into me garden an' looks out o'er th' river, an' well I sees ut, not bein' loike them what shuts therselves up, an' cain't even stan' in front o' a drop o' good rine. An' th' wind's right, an' th' toide's right, an' I count th' place they calls 'Olland ain't bin shifted. If ther was 'arf th' pluck ther used to be when I wor a lad, they'd be out wi' th' boats, an' ye 'd see some o' they big-sail'd luggers a-turnin' in fr' th' main, an' all th' stuff o'erboard down be Cripple's Creek, an' th' lights a-shinin', an' th' horses a-gallopin', an' folk lookin' out o' th' winders, though they dussent never show n' lights. Ah, they was a foine set o' min, an we shaint see th' likes o' they in these parts agin. They din't goo arter ducks and dabs, like th' fools they've left behind 'em. All dead like they air, an' gone, an I'll be gooin' soon, an' no mistake, bein' wery, wery old an' toired like.' *Its familiar Features*

S. L. Bensusan,
A Country-side Chronicle, 1907.

The Beauty of the Marshes

A MORE desolate region can scarce be conceived, and yet it is not without beauty. In summer the thrift mantles the marshes with shot satin, passing through all gradations of tint from maiden's blush to lily white. Thereafter a purple glow steals over the water as the sea-lavender bursts into flower, and simultaneously every creek and pool is royally fringed with sea-aster. A little later the glasswort, that shot up green and transparent as emerald glass in the early spring, turns to every tinge of carmine. When all vegetation ceases to live and goes to sleep, the marshes are alive and wakeful with countless wild fowl. At all times they are haunted with seamews and Royston crows, in winter they teem with wild duck and grey geese. The stately heron loves to wade in the pools, occasionally the whooper swan sounds his loud trumpet, and flashes a white reflection in the still blue waters of the fleets. The plaintive pipe of the curlew is familiar to those who frequent these marshes, and the barking of the Brent geese as they return from their northern breeding-places is heard in November. . . .

The sea is not here what it is on other coasts—foaming, colour-shifting, like a peacock's neck: here it is of one tone and grey, and never tosses in waves, but creeps in like a thief over the shallow mud-flat, and babbles like a dotard over the mean shells and clots of weed on our strand.

S. BARING-GOULD, *Mehalah*, 1880.

Once thought unhealthy

I HAVE one remark before I leave this damp part of the world . . . that I took notice of a strange decay of the sex here, insomuch that it was very frequent to meet with men that had had from five or six to fourteen or fifteen wives, nay, and some more. . . The reason as a merry fellow told me was this: that they, being bred in the marshes themselves and seasoned to the place, did pretty well, but that they always went up into the uplands for a wife. That when they took the young lasses out of the wholesome, fresh air they were healthy but they presently changed complexion, got an ague or two, and seldom held it above half a year, or a year at most. 'And then,' said he, 'we go to the uplands again and fetch another,' so that marrying of wives was reckoned a kind of good farm to them.

DANIEL DEFOE,
A Tour through Great Britain, 1722.

Dengie Marshes

Its familiar Features

THE view looking over the Dengie Flats and St. Peter's Sands from the summit of the earthen bank which keeps out the sea, was very desolate and strange. Behind us lay a vast, drear expanse of land won from the ocean in days bygone, bordered on the one side by the Blackwater, and on the other by the Crouch River, and saved none too well from the mastery of the waves by the sloping earthen bank on which we stood. In front, thousands of acres of grey mud where grew dull, unwholesome looking grasses. Far, far away on this waste, two tiny, moving specks, men engaged in seeking for samphire, or some other treasure of the ooze-mud. Then the thin, white lip of the sea and beyond its sapphire edge in the half-distance the gaunt skeleton of a long-wrecked ship. To the north, on the horizon a line of trees ; to the west, over the great plain, where stood one or two lonely farms, another line of trees. On the distant deep some sails, and in the middle marsh, a barge gliding up a hidden creek as though she moved across the solid land. Then, spread like a golden garment over the vast expanses of earth and ocean, the flood of sunshine, and in our ears the rush of the north-west gale, and the thrilling song of larks hanging high above the yellow, salt-soaked fields. Such seemed the Dengie Marsh as I saw it in June 1901. But what must it be like when buried beneath the snows of winter, or when the howling easterly winds of spring sweep across its spaces, and the combers of the North Sea sometimes reach and batter their frail embankment? Then, indeed, I should not like to be the tenant of one of those solitary steads.

H. RIDER HAGGARD, *Rural England*, 1902.

Shrimping at Leigh

Its familiar Features

A GLANCE at the map shows where Leigh stands, on the sunny slope of a hill at the head of a bight formed by the line of Essex Coast and the eastern shore of Canvey Island, where the estuary of the Thames abruptly widens out from two miles to four miles in breadth, with a stretch of sands and mud dry at low water, reaching along the north shore of the river as far as Southend. The view of Leigh from the water is very picturesque, a foreground of fishing bawleys, a line of straggling cottages along Leigh Creek, backed by others rising in tiers irregularly one above the other, with bright red-tiled roofs and green trees and gardens, and the church at the top of the hill, and near to it a grove of elms where the rooks build and clamour all through the spring and early summer. . . .

The inhabitants of Leigh are nearly all fishermen and their vessels, which are called bawleys, are cutters of about twenty tons, drawing six feet of water, clinker built, and with mainsails of great hoist, with long gaffs and no booms. There are over a hundred of these craft and they make a brave show in Sea Reach, as they trawl under topsail, foresail and braided mainsail. It is a very pretty sight to see them starting off in the grey of the morning, or coming home in the afternoon with their shrimps boiling, or being packed all ready for market. . . . The bawleys lie at anchor in the Ray, and from a distance seem to form a regular forest of masts all along the channel. Here they lie afloat at all tides, and the fishermen go to and from them in their punts or footboats, over the flats or down to Leigh Creek. Often, as they come up the creek with the first of the flood, the boats crowd along in a densely packed mass, now sticking fast aground and now floating on again as the tide rises, each boat with its two or three hampers of shrimps packed and labelled in readiness for the train. They boil their shrimps while under weigh, each vessel carrying a copper for the purpose ; and the shrimps as soon as caught are cast into a seething cauldron of strong brine—salt water with lumps of salt dissolved in it. This makes the shrimp dry and crisp, and imparts that special salt flavour which makes him harmonise so well with tea and watercress, at ninepence a head.

Its familiar Features

H. Lewis Jones,
Swin, Swale and Swatchway, 1892.

Canvey Island

No one who has not visited Canvey would believe that so lonely and out-of-the-world a spot could be discovered at a distance of thirty miles from London. Just as we sometimes find—within half a dozen paces of a great city thoroughfare, where the black and pursuing streams of passengers who throng its pavements never cease to flow, and where the roar of traffic is never still—some silent and unsuspected alley or court into which no stranger turns aside, so, bordering the great world-thoroughfare of the Thames is to be found a spot where life seems stagnant, and where scarcely one of the thousands who pass within a stone's throw has ever set foot.

Where the Thames swings round within sight of the sea, there lies, well out of the sweep of the current, a pear-shaped island, some six miles long and three miles broad, which is known as Canvey.

Three hundred years ago it was practically uninhabitable. At high tide the marshes were flooded, and it was not until 1623 that James I. invited a Dutchman named Joas Croppenburgh to

Its familiar Features settle there, offering him a third for himself if he could reclaim the island from the sea. This offer the enterprising Dutchman accepted, and immediately set to work to build a sea wall, which effectually protects the low-lying marsh-land, that, standing inside the wall, one seems to be at a lower level than the water, and can see only the topmost spars and sails of the, apparently, bodiless barges and boats that glide ghostlike by.

The evil-looking dynamite hulks, which lie scowling on the water, like huge red coffins, are the most noticeable feature in the scenery of Canvey. Upwards of a dozen of these nests of devilry are moored off the island, and are the first objects to catch the eye as one looks out from the sea-wall.

In view of the fact that the position of Canvey, in regard to one of the greatest water highways in the world, is like that of a house which lies only a few yards back from a main road,—one wonders at first that such a locality should have been selected as the storage place of so vast a quantity of a deadly explosive. That it was so selected, only after the matter had received the most careful and serious consideration of the authorities, is certain; and though very nearly the whole of the shipping which enters the Thames must necessarily pass almost within hail of the island, the spot is so remote and out of the way that it is doubtful if any safer or securer place could have been found.

COULSON KERNAHAN, *Captain Shannon*, 1897.

An Open Question

The Red Hills MEHALAH waited till evening, then she wrapped a cloak round her, put her pistol in her belt and walked through the marsh to the point indicated by the shepherd as the Burnt Hill. Through all the low flat coast-land of this region, above the saltings or pasture overflowed by high tides, occasionally are scattered at irregular intervals large broad circular mounds of clay burned to brick red, interspersed with particles of charcoal. A few fragments of bone are found in them, relics of the meals of those who raised these heaps, but they cover no urns, and enclose no cists, they contain no skeletons. They were never intended as funeral monuments, and are quite different from the hoes or barrows which stand on high land, and which were burial mounds. The burnt or red hills are always situate at high water mark ; near them below the surface of the vegetable deposit, are multitudes of oyster shells. Who raised these mounds? For what purpose were they reared? These are questions which cannot be answered satisfactorily. One thing is certain. An immense amount of wood must have been consumed to burn such a mass of clay, and the country must then have been more overgrown with timber than at present. Many of the mounds are now enclosed in fields by sea-walls which hold out the tide, the plough has been drawn over them, and the spade has scattered them over the surface, colouring a whole field brick red, and making it rich for the production of corn. There is no better manure than a red hill.

A cold east wind wailed over the waste ; a white fog like curd lay on the water and the surface of the saltings, clinging to the surface and rising scarce above three feet from it. Above the sky was clear, and a fine crescent moon sparkled in it without quenching the keenness of the stars. Cassiopeia was glorious in her chair, Orion burned sideways over Mersea Isle. To the north-west was a silvery glow at the horizon, then there rose a pure ray as of returning daylight, it was answered by a throb in the north-east, then it broke into two rays, and again united and spread, and suddenly was withdrawn. Mehalah had often seen the Aurora and she knew the signals portended cold or bad weather.

S. BARING-GOULD, *Mehalah.*

THE mystery of the Red Hills still remains, notwithstanding many rival theories, as profound as ever.

HORACE WILMER,
(Hon. Sec. Exploration Committee), (1910).

Across the River

THE Blackwater estuary stretches far and wide beyond the meadow, and at times of the year like the present, when 'longen folk to gon on pilgrimages,' I am filled with a keen desire to travel. Not to go abroad, not to journey to some sun-stricken town in a far-off land where the civilization we know best is not, but to cross the shining estuary and explore the villages on the far side of the river. I have travelled, have been north and south, and east to the isles of the sea; certain far lands and wild peoples are no longer strange to me, but the mysterious country across the estuary enshrines more possibilities than Tibet. The sun lights up tiny villages set amid prosperous fields, a telescope brings them seemingly within reach, but I am no nearer. Villagers who have passed more than eighty years on this side of the Blackwater have never been across the estuary; there are strong tides, dangerous currents, sandbanks, impediments innumerable. Though the river narrows rapidly a mile or two further inland, the only bridge across it is nearly fifteen miles away, amid the peaceful streets of the market-town. . . . Folk have told me that there is an old wildfowl decoy over there, at a point nearly opposite my cottage. . . . They say the nightingales nest in a favoured clump of laurel and thorn by the decoy; that blackcaps, woodlarks and thrushes help to make the finest choir the county holds. Great flights of plover, golden and green, are to be found in the meadows by the waterside. . . . Some of the villagers possess curious relics turned up by the plough in early years of the last century, and brought across the water in the old smuggling days. They tell me there is much to reward the antiquary as well as the naturalist.

Then why not cross the river? I ask myself the question at all seasons of the year, when the orchard blossoms, when the bees are humming in the chestnut-trees, when the first hay crop is taken, when the partridge falls on the stubble, when the wild geese come in on the wings of the north-east wind. I ask, and find no answer, for I will not tell myself the truth. Deep down in my heart I know that fear keeps me on this side of the estuary. Do not misunderstand me. Some local Palinurus could be found to steer me safely across, or I could ride to the market town and go down on the other bank of the river. It would be no more than a summer day's jaunt. My one fear is disenchantment. Suppose my expectations should not be realised? Why should I risk a statement that the nightingales have left the laurel plantation; that the wild-fowl no longer nest in the sedges; that the moat is filled, and the moated house modernized. What would be left to care about if they told me that some land company is going to sell the plover-thronged meadows in plots 'suitable for the erection of villas,' or that a railway line is to be brought to the village that has never heard the sound of an engine whistle.

Better far to stay on my side of the river, and

watch the barges going up or down with the tide, or study the heavy flight of the herons, and look out for the V-shaped phalanx of the wild duck. Best to admire my enchanted land through the telescope, to accept the stories and traditions current here, and leave the Blackwater between me and the country of my dreams.

S. L. Bensusan, *A Countryside Chronicle.*

OUR FARMS, VILLAGES AND FLORA

Greene rye in September when timely thou hast,
October for weat sowing calleth as fast.
If weather will suffer, this council I geue
Leaue sowing of wheat before Hallowmas eve.

Where wheat upon edish ye mind to bestow,
Let that be the first of the wheat ye do sow.
He seemeth to hart it and comfort to bring:
That gyveth it comfort of Michaelmas spring.

Whight wheat upon pease etch is willing to grow,
Though best upon fallow as many do know.
But where, how, or when, ye entend to begin:
Let euer the finest be first sowen in.

THOMAS TUSSER, *October's Husbandry.*

Dry seas, with golden surges, ebb and flow;
The ripening ears smile as we go,
With boasts to crack the barn, so numberless they show.

EDWARD BENLOWES, *The Sweetness of Retirement.*

ESSEX has long been famous for containing some of the largest farms in the kingdom. . . . Viewing the county in general, the size of farms is very moderate ; in all the interior of the county, four or five hundred acres are a large farm ; and the number of much smaller ones very great.

Farms and Farmsteads

ARTHUR YOUNG,
Agricultural Survey of Essex, 1807.

Work of the Farm

BRIGHT glows the east with blushing red,
While yet upon their homely bed
The sleeping labourers rest ;
And the pale moon and silver star
Grow paler still, and wandering far,
Sink slowly to the west.

And see behind the sloping hill,
The morning clouds grow brighter still,
And all the shades retire ;
Slowly the sun, with golden ray,
Breaks forth above the horizon grey,
And gilds the distant spire.

And now at Nature's cheerful voice,
The hills and vales and woods rejoice,
The lark ascends the skies ;
And soon the cock's shrill notes alarm
The sleeping people of the farm,
And bid them all arise.

Then at the dairy's cool retreat
The busy maids and mistress meet,
The early hours to seize ;
Some tend with skilful hand the churns,
Where the thick cream to butter turns,
And some the curdling cheese.

And now comes Thomas from the house,
With well-known cry to call the cows,
Still resting on the plain;
They quickly rising, one and all,
Obedient to the daily call,
Wind slowly through the lane.

And see the rosy milkmaid now,
Seated beside the hornëd cow,
With milking stool and pail;
The patient cow, with dappled hide,
Stands still, unless to lash her side
With her convenient tail.

And then the poultry (Mary's charge)
Must all be fed and let at large,
To roam about again;
Wide open springs the great barn door,
And out the hungry creatures pour,
To pick the scattered grain.

The sun-burnt labourer hastens now
To plod behind the heavy plough,
And guide with skilful arm;
Thus all is industry around,
No idle hand is ever found,
Within the busy farm.

JANE TAYLOR, *Original Poems*, 1804.

'Spirit o' the Farm'

(*In the black days of* 1883).

IT is a dreary sight, these fields out of cultivation, with the edges, once so jealously guarded, now broken down, and the clusters of weeds that sparsely hide the cold pale ground beneath. Nature has not yet claimed her own, for here and there 'mid the weeds of thistles, charlock, henbane and poppy, the old favourites of man look out sorrowfully, like friends in adversity, neglected, and even the passing winds sigh mournfully.

Oh, yes, I have had lots of reasons given, one gentleman told me that this land should never have been tilled at all, and that there's lots more would go out same as this has done. It was a bad sign for the people, he said, when land like this could be farmed at a profit, and perhaps he was right. Anyway, bread don't seem much cheaper with wheat at 17s. than what it was at 27s., and labourers hard to get with the farms going out and all. 'Well, of course, there's always been a deal of gatting about bad landlords, and maybe landlords is a bit hard here and there; only when the rent falls below the tithe it don't seem much use this sort of talk; but bless you, its all in politics and commissions and the like. You'll find it all there with one a-talking of high farming, another of compensation: and I don't know what they will compensate for, unless it be for farming the land at all with wheat at 17s. 6d.'

'Yet I've heard plenty say we never kept up with the new ideas here—drifted behind, as it were. 'Tis all in the say, but I never could get to think much of it. Many's the time I've been up and down this very field with bits of new machines and things. Now it was a new sort of artificial, now 'twas a new turnip topper, with half the turnips behind cut in two, cruel, and never touched the bottom at all. I mind well the old master was always ready to take and try with anything new, till it came to having rails in the stackyard which he wouldn't, but little good he ever took from the few of them. And with them artificials 'twas much the same. For the land's just like a child, and the more you give the more 'twill expect, and sort o' run sulky without. Times you could a'most see the crop a-growing, and then next crop would be left on the ground, all because of them salts, powders and messes. Maybe we didn't mix 'em right, but anyway, there it was, and no good a-talking.'

These lands are strange to us, let us on, on to the golden cornfields in the wake of the western sun. What are these dull cold fields to us? But for this old labourer they are full of memories—memories of good times, of lively bustle and contentment when through the yard the men would lead the great cart-horses to and from their work, and the voice of the old farmer rang out cheerily in the early morn as he bade 'God save you' to his good wife on his way to market. 'Ah! This was years ago,' he will tell you, 'and now the lands are gone to waste, are fit for naught, and the old farmhouse is a ruin, the windows broken in, and all quiet, just like a picture.'

'Well, sir, 'tis a hard question. I think it's the soul has left the land. 'Tis what the old farmer said to me, "The spirit o' the farm has gone," he said, "and 'tis time I was a-leaving." That he said to me, and never lived long, but many's the time it's come back to me sort o' true, and I can't help but believe it.'

'Well, good-night to you.'

'Good-night, sir.'

H. Cranmer-Byng, *A Romance of the Fair*, 1897.

Life on an Essex Farm Sixty Years Ago

THOSE were the days of the smock frock—a worn and shabby one for every day, a better one, of a soft greenish hue, for Sundays. This in its turn descended to the weekday wear, and very likely to another and a third generation. The smock was a comprehensive garment that reached below the knees, the farm labourer's lower extremities being cased on Sundays in short brown leather buskins, which met the hem of the smock. The wives of the farm men appeared on Sundays in large circular cloaks that enveloped their spare figures. At the time of which I am writing, scarlet ones were getting few and far between, but the little bit of colour seen across the common under the ancient lime trees was a most picturesque sight.

Implements were then very scarce upon the farms. Hardly any of the farmers had even drills of their own. To possess a drill, or more than one, and to take it round the neighbourhood, or let it out to farmers, was a trade in itself. . . . All the wheat was threshed by a flail upon the barn floors, and comfortable warm work it was during the long, cold winter. The flop-flop of the flails is still as fresh as possible in my memory.

Those who only have to pay a penny for their letters to any part of the United Kingdom, or the Colonies, would perhaps have grudged the five-pence necessary to frank a letter from Braintree to Chelmsford. Three times only in a week did letters find their way to our village, from which year after year a weather-beaten old dame travelled on foot to the town and back, laden with many things besides letters. One winter morning early she was found frozen to death in the Watery Lane. There was no putting out of washing in those days, but every farmhouse had its grand washing days, when the women started work at four o'clock in the morning, indeed some of them came over night. Strange as it may seem now, they would stand all day at the wash-tub or copper, rubbing and wringing (there were no wringing machines), and would go home at night well satisfied with receiving something under a shilling, and their meals.

The game on our farm was carefully preserved by the landlord, whose visits we children highly appreciated, for the sake of the brand new shillings or sixpences which the old banker brought in his pocket from Lombard Street. He was invariably dressed in a light, short jacket reaching only to the waist, and worn outside his coat. This garment was called a spencer, after Earl Spencer, who, as Lord Althorp, had been Chancellor of the Exchequer in 1830. . . . If the old landlord came in his whiskey (a light, two-wheeled conveyance for one horse, made for quick travelling, hence its name) we were more than delighted, especially if he drove in it the horse that had such an appropriate name. Brought to his stables one day, when he was in his most decisive mood, he had scarcely cast eyes upon it before rapping out in his abrupt way: 'What's the price?' 'Fifty guineas,' said the owner promptly. 'I'll have it,' came as quickly in reply, and the animal was forthwith named Moment. His coachman at the same time was one Moses, and the old Squire's order: 'Tell Moses to put Moment into the whiskey,' which we children heard repeated, seemed to us of almost biblical importance. These are only a few rambling reminiscences of sixty years ago, but yet enough to show the rising generation in what a different age from that of our childhood they have opened their eyes.

S.S., *Essex Review*, 1900.

Life on a Farm

UP in the morning early,
Not quite so early to bed;
The foot may be light,
From haste or delight,
But it's wonderful heavy to tread.

Seed-time as well as harvest,
  Winter as well as spring;
    True! rest may be found,
    But to live off the ground,
  And find it's a different thing.

Sowing, hoeing and mowing,
  Drilling, dressing and drains,
    So cumber the mind,
    One seldom can find
  Any leisure except when it rains.

Weeds, worry and work,
  Muck, money and mares;
    Oh, for the hour
    That shall quell the power
  Of the working farmer's cares.

Indoors as well as out,
  The thronging duties come;
    Little's the peace
    Or the quietness,
  In the working farmer's home.

But I may not longer dwell
  On the worry of farming life;
    For I fear 'tis clear
    That the singer here
  Is a working farmer's wife.

M. A. CHAPLIN, *Sunlit Spray*, 1898.

The Flail

EVEN now in some parts of England, the flail does its work, and the writer's observation and correspondence with responsible persons in many quarters, offers reason to believe that it will be a long time before the small farmer will resign it in favour of other and more up-to-date methods. Not on sentimental grounds, but because it is obvious that on a moderate-sized holding, where few cereals are grown, or where they are cultivated in comparatively inconsiderable quantities, it would not pay to send the corn to be threshed elsewhere, or to hire a machine to thresh it on the farm. Inquiries show that the flail is still being made in several of our shires, including Essex, and the instrument of to-day is practically the same as that represented in mediæval drawings, although in the Middle Ages it was perhaps somewhat longer in the handle. . . . Its survival into the twentieth century links up the age of steam and electricity with those remote days when pilgrims ambled to Canterbury and gossipped as they rode ; while its gradual passing into disuse pathetically points a moral and adorns the fateful tale of English agriculture. The place of the thresher, flail in hand, in the pastoral scene, possesses a charm that has made its appeal alike to J. F. Millet, the artist, and Robert Burns, the poet. Memory loves to dwell on the picture of the happy homestead where

> 'An old barn gable end was seen,
> Sprinkled with Nature's mossy green,
> Hard on the right, from where the flail
> Of thresher sounded down the vale.'

H. W. LEWER, *Essex Review*, 1908.

The Farm Labourer

IT has long been the custom, I am aware, to look down from a superior height upon the agricultural workman, to call him Hodge, and to credit him with little more intelligence than the beasts he litters or the turnips he pulls to feed them.

But compare him with the mechanic employed in a factory whose tending of a certain machine varies, perhaps, not a hair's breadth from day to day, year in and year out, and you will perchance appreciate his superior range of gifts. As season succeeds season, one avocation is laid aside for another, and whether it is hoeing gingerly between rows of green springing corn, pulling and clamping roots for winter store, felling timber, bush-harrowing pastures or spreading manure, he is expected to be a past master in each art. Only the shepherd, the stockman, the carpenter and thatcher are specialists in their own particular line, and often the ordinary labourer may be called to take his turn at one or other of these avocations of the superior workman.

I never watch the building of a barley rick (tied corn is easier), or even the topping-up of a loaded waggon of hay, without marvelling at the precision of form attained by these simple rustics, ignorant of the very alphabet of Euclid. I cannot see them laying open a field for draining, cutting the ditches, adjusting the pipes to the fall of the surface, and covering them with a loose layer of bushes, without pondering upon their absolute innocence of all the laws of hydrostatics. And when it comes to striking furrows across a newly ploughed ten-acre bit, I am fairly lost in amazement at the unerring eye and mathematical precision of aim which steer the huge unwieldly cart-horses down the diagonal line from point to point. It is this manifold direction of effort, this manysidedness of his calling, solitary with nature and under the wide skies, that rouses all the dormant possibilities in his slow nature, and makes the really observant farm labourer the most interesting creature of the peasant class to talk to in his old age.

CHARLOTTE FELL SMITH, *Land Magazine*, 1898.

Harvest Time

THE various fields display the mellowing corn,
And crouding crops the labour'd soil adorn.
These labour'd fields may boast the various grain,
That smiling bend, and tempt the reaping train :
On many a spot the russet wheat appears,
The staff of life, and prop of human years ;
The bladed barley, arm'd with many a dart,
Whose generous dregs revive the poor man's heart ;
The slender oat, that shoots and blooms on high ;
And borne by tapering stems the waving rye :
In some the broad and juicy turnip grows ;
The creeping pea ; the bean that sweetly blows ;
The clover green, whose velvet leaves are spread
Close to the earth beneath its purple head.

W. HURN, *Heath Hill, Dedham*, 1777.

Essex Wheat and Roses

FROM her rich-sucking lips of deep-dyed clay
Red bubbles blows she of a summer's day—
Roses how light and sweet !
From out her heavy head of dense brown mould
Shoot Samson locks of airy fiery gold—
Was ever grown such wheat ?

ARTHUR SHEARLEY CRIPPS, (1911).

The Dream-barn

OFT in the shadows of my barn I sit,
Watching the sunbeams play at hide and seek,
While silken cobwebs brush against my cheek,
And stealthy sparrows through the top lights flit ;

And in the dreamful silence of the corn,
I hear their lasting requiem from toil,
Who were the sons and wooers of the soil,
Lords of the golden harvest of the morn.

Sunlight and Shadow, hoarded grain and dust,
And the low whirr of little pirate wings
Of such the autumn of a heart, that sings,
Only because, like Philomel, she must ;
Till love comes shyly through the crevice thrust,
A rose that yields the perfume of strange springs.

L. CRANMER-BYNG, *An English Rose, &c.*

Maldon

DURING the early part of the unquiet tenth century it is believed that Mersea, the Sokens, the only part of Essex where Danish names still linger, and the Blackwater estuary were the headquarters of the Danes in England. Maldon was then the first important entrenchment to be overcome when they made their frequent inland incursions. In the reign of Ethelred II. (the Unready) the *Saxon Chronicle* records—'This year came Unlaf with 93 ships to Staines and laid waste all around, and thence he went to Sandwich, and thence to Gypswic [Ipswich], and harried it all, and so to Maeldune ; and then Brythnoth, the Ealdorman and his force came against him and fought with him, and there they slew the Ealdorman and kept the battlefield.' The battle lasted fourteen days and is described in an almost contemporaneous fragment, said by E. A. Freeman to rank among the noblest efforts of Teutonic poetry.

EDWARD A. FITCH,
Maldon and the River Blackwater, 1871.

TOTHAM, what minstrel ever sung of thee,
  Thou peaceful rustic dear enchanting spot?
  To thee inscribed whoe'er a lay did see?
  Egregious bards! Thou 'st been by all forgot;
But thou no longer shall thus slighted be—
Totham! my feeble muse shall sing of thee.

Hail then, old Totham, spot unknown to fame—
  Hail to thee, basking in thy 'pride of place,'
Thy beauteous scenes must every breast inflame,
  And leave impressions time can ne'er efface.
The hills, the vales, all that we view in thee,
Are deck'd in Nature's choicest livery.

How changed since thou, in days of other years,
  Wert but a wild, almost unpeopled spot—
Since folks on thee were wont to pass their jeers;
  'Cold Tiptree Heath,' they dubbed thee, and thy lot
'Twas to be deem'd condemned as nothing less
Than the abode of sickness and distress.

'Salubrious Totham'—that thou 'rt deemëd now,
  And thy pure zephyrs all delight to inhale.
But thy grand prospects, Totham, words, oh how
  Can they pourtray the beauties of the vale
Spread south of thee! a vast, a gorgeous view
Of landscape—the ever charming, ever new.

Blackwater's Bay, graced with the passing bark,
  Its glistening tide a mirror to Sol's rays,
Majestic hills, rich vales, groves still and dark,
  And old Maeldune, so famed in ancient days,
All these are seen, ye travellers, if you will
But wend your way to Totham's Beacon Hill.

Ye Essex hills, though high your summits are,
  Ye heights of Laindon, Danbury and all
To Beacon Hill, so exquisitely fair,
  Ye are but pigmies to a giant tall.

A cloud oblivious o'er your face it spreads—
Ye must to it 'hide your diminished heads.'

From its proud height when warlike scenes were rife
  The startling beacon's blaze was to have flared ;
But God be praised ! from dire invasion's strife
  Britannia's sea-environed land was spared :
None ventured, spite of danger and of death,
To rob our brow of the war laurelled wreath.

War, fiendlike war, yes e'en old Totham's plains
  Have been the scene of thee. In days of yore,
Unyielding Saxons and invading Danes,
  In conflict, have her sod stain'd with their gore,
And through her now still shades have echoed far
The shouts of armies at the tug of war.

The names of Wulfmor and of stern Brithnoth
  On Valour's roll should stand among the first :
What glorious bravery was shown by both !
  From Brithnoth's lips the chieftain's orders burst
E'en till his wound threw him into Death's trance
The well-tim'd order was 'Advance ! Advance !'

*   *   *   *

Totham, farewell ! I'll sing no more of thee,
  None but a Byron should sing in thy praise ;
A warm admirer, know, thou hast in me,
  And I my best have done thy fame to raise.
Again, farewell—your bard but wishes he
Had power to inscribe a worthier lay to thee.

CHARLES CLARK.

Stifford

THE very names of some of the parishes in our neighbourhood show that, valuable as every acre is now, and many and well worn as our roads are now, it was in the British and early Anglo-Saxon times a part of the huge

Essex forest, with only a clearing at distant intervals for supplying the few necessaries of savage life. A rural poet, of no common merit, has described Stifford and its neighbourhood of those days thus, and its transition :—

'Then branching horns appeared o'er branching
ferns ;
And wolves, more rare and wary year by year,
Slunk through the glades, till hunger made them
bold.
Then wild boars crunched the acorns as they fell ;
Or ploughed the earth for roots with ivory share.
But plot by plot the forest lost and lost,
As red men yield to white. The moated hall
With lofty chimneys rose, and mighty roofs
Which spanned the hall where lord and villein
supped.
As years rolled on the tenant filled the place
Of him who owned the soil, while still the poor
Received and cheerful paid the old regards ;
And to their native fields contented clung.'

WILLIAM PALIN,
Stifford and its Neighbourhood, 1871.

Stambourne

CERTAIN up and down roads, with broad margins of green, and walls of hedge ; ponds as brown and foul as stale beer ; ducks and goslings *ad lib.* ; plots of woodland ; fields of 'tarmuts' and 'wuzzel,' oats and barley ; a windmill ; two or three nice houses, with gardens and lawns ; numbers of cottages, which could hardly be less picturesque ; great wealth of fine trees ; stretches of meadow land ;

valleys and undulations; pigs and donkeys; and, withal, a general disorderliness of fertility, and a sense of being out of the world and having nothing particular to do, and you are getting an idea of *Stambourne.*

C. H. SPURGEON, *Memories of Stambourne*, 1892.

Stambourne Parsonage

IN my grandfather's garden there were two arbours made of yew trees, cut into sugar-loaf fashion, and a fine old hedge of yew, of considerable length, which was clipped and trimmed till it was quite a wall of verdure. Behind it was a wide grass walk, which looked upon the fields; the grass was kept mown, so as to make pleasant walking. Here, ever since the old Puritanic chapel was built [1676], godly divines had walked and prayed and meditated. My grandfather was wont to use it as his study. Up and down it he would walk when preparing his sermons, and always on Sabbath days, when it was fair, he would have half an hour there before preaching. To me, it seemed to be a perfect paradise; and being forbidden to stay there when grandfather was meditating, I viewed it with no small degree of awe. I love to think of the green and quiet walk at this moment; but I was once shocked and even horrified by hearing a farming man remark concerning this *sanctum sanctorum*: 'It 'ud grow a many 'taturs if it wor plowed up.'

C. H. SPURGEON, *Autobiography*, 1897.

HAVE you never heard of Birdbrook—name musical with sweet voices of flowing runnels and flitting songsters, surrounded with bowers of rushes, sedges, bushes, brambles and climbing honeysuckle? And there is Ridgewell:

the Romans there, or thereabouts, had quite a notable settlement. Do you not know Toppesfield and Wethersfield, and Finchingfield and Bardfield? Are all these villages fresh fields to you? Are you so obscure as not to have heard of Sturmer and Helions Bumpstead? Must we give you up? We certainly shall if the august name of Steeple Bumpstead has never bumped against your memory. Hempstead we will not insist upon, though Dick Turpin was born there; for there seems to have been a Hempstead everywhere in days when hemp was the great vindicator of justice, and stood the magistrate in such excellent stead; when men would not be converted by the stocks, nor be sanctified by being whipped at the cart-tail. Harvey, the great Harvey, sleeps in pieces in the church of the aforenamed Hempstead; but it may be that your blood has circulated for years without your knowing who first discovered the fact. But then, you have a cousin living at Great Yeldham! Have you not? Surely, Yeldham Great Oak must have been one of the visions of your youth, and it must abide among the memories of your riper years. No? Not know Great Yeldham? Go to! Prisoner in some vast furnace of smoke, which is called a city, what knowest thou of the freshest, greenest, purest things which yet linger under the sun?

C. H. SPURGEON, *Memories of Stambourne.*

Felsted

AT Felsted's village, neat and small,
Whose church-tower rises grey and tall,
Still stands an ancient dwelling there,
Of strange device and carving rare.
Now partly lost 'neath patch and paint.
Retaining still a legend quaint,

In letters old with grand parade,
Which tell by whom THIS HOUSE WAS MADE.

* * * *

There is a rich and mossy dell,
Where loves the nightingale to dwell,
'Twixt Camsix Farm and Hartford End,
Through which a stream is seen to wend,
'Midst trees that rise on either bank,
With reeds and rushes coarse and dank,
And steals along so still and slow,
That one can scarcely mark its flow,
Save by the leaves that on it lie
In Autumn, ever floating by;
As when, with youth's bright sunshine gay,
We mark the friends that pass away,
And only think, when they are gone,
That unperceiv'd thus time steals on.

GEORGE T. MANNING, *Rural Rhymes*, 1837.

Stebbing

MANY of the Stebbing farm-houses, lying far from the roadside, and surrounded with a moat, must be pretty much the same as when, in the time of the seventeenth century persecutions, persons meeting for worship fastened the doors, stationed the sentinels, and omitted the song of praise which should declare the presence of a company of worshippers whose sole transgression against the law was that they claimed the right to worship otherwise than in accord with the teachings of the Book of Common Prayer. Among the worshippers who then braved the dangers of fine and imprisonment, were dwellers, if not in the very same labourers' cottages that we see now, yet in cottages built in similar style, of plaister and wood, with thatched roofs and gable ends. W. H. BECKETT,

Free Church Life in Stebbing, 1893.

Mistley

THE smoaking town ; the port ; the cottage
small ;
The marshy ooze ; the antiquated hall ;
The curious bridge, high arch'd and white as snow ;
The rushy flat, the ragged hedge below ;
The bushy hollow of the slanting hill ;
The crumbling marge blue-bending o'er the rill ;
The valley deep below the dusky wood ;
The mill that pours in cataracts the flood ;
And many an ancient steeple's hoary head,
That looks with reverence o'er the rustic dead.
Pleas'd could I, Mistley, thro' thy hamlet stray,
Where the green park unveils the grass-rob'd way,
And pleas'd depict the beauties that surround
Thy lovely structure on the smooth-mown ground,
Did not the swelling hills on every side
Break my exploring view in envious pride ;
Did not the trees that on the hills arise
Hide you, sweet gardens, from my searching eyes.

WILLIAM HURN, *Heath Hill.*

Chigwell

(*Revisited after fifty years' absence.*)

DEPUTED by the tuneful nine,
A Pilgrim to an Eastern shrine
I once again out-sally ;
Again to Chigwell wander back,
And, more excursive, aim to track
Each neighbouring hill and valley.

Strange that a village should survive
For ten years multiplied by five

The same in size and figure.
Knowing nor plenty nor distress,
If foiled by fortune, why no less?
If favoured, why no bigger?

Say why has population got
Spellbound upon this level spot,
Undamaged by profusion?
A tyro, I the question ask;
Be thine, Miss Martineau, the task
To tender the solution.

I pass the vicar's white abode,
And pond'ring, gain the upward road,
By busy thoughts o'erladen.
To where the pride of Chigwell Row
Still lives—a handsome widow now,
As erst a lovely maiden.

Here hills and dales and distant Thame,
And forest glens, green proof proclaim,
Of Nature's lavish bounty;
And dub thee, lofty region, still,
Surrey's tall foe, the Richmond Hill,
Of this our eastern county.

Diverging from the road, the sod
I tread that once a boy I trod,
With pace not quite so nimble;
But where's the Maypole next the lane?
Who dared to banish from the plain
That wreath-encircled symbol?

Abridge, her tank and waterfall,
The path beneath Sir Eliab's wall,
I once again am stepping,
Beyond that round we rarely stirr'd,
Loughton we saw—but only heard
Of Ongar and of Epping.

Seek we the river's grassy verge,
Where all were destined to immerge,

Or willing, or abhorrent ;
I view the well-known mill-hole still,
But time has dwindled to a rill,
What seem'd of yore, a torrent.

Here, fell destroyer, many a wound,
The woodman's axe has dealt around,
Lee Grove in death reposes.
Yet while her dryads seek their tombs,
The miller's moated garden blooms,
With all its wonted roses.

* * * *

Twilight steals on. I wander back,
The listless ploughman's homeward track
Again in thought I follow ;
Or sit the antique porch within,
Awed by the belfry's deafening din,
And watch the wheeling swallow.

Chigwell, I cease thy charms to sing,
Time bears me elsewhere on his wing.
Perhaps, ere long, the poet
Who now, in mental vigour bold,
Parades erect thy churchyard mould,
May sleep, supine, below it.

So let it be : Time, take thy course ;
Let dotards with tenacious force
Cling to this waning planet ;
I'd rather soar to death's abode
On angels' wings than live a toad,
Pent in a block of granite.

* * * *

I fear not, Fate, thy pendent shears,
There are, who pray for length of years,
To them, not me, allot 'em.
Life's cup is nectar at the brink,
Midway a palatable drink,
And wormwood at the bottom.

JAMES SMITH, *Life*, 1839.

Walthamstow in 1840

EASTWARD and landward it is all flat pasture, once marsh, except for a few gardens, and there are very few permanent dwellings there, scarcely anything but a few sheds and cots for the men who come to look after the great herds of cattle. What with the beasts and the men, and the scattered red-tiled roofs and the big hay-ricks, it does not make a bad holiday to get a quiet pony and ride about there on a sunny afternoon of autumn, and look over the river and the craft passing up and down, and on to Shooter's Hill and the Kentish Uplands, and then turn round to the wide green sea of the Essex marshland, with the great domed line of the sky, and the sun shining down in one flood of peaceful light over the long distance.

WILLIAM MORRIS, *News from Nowhere*, 1890.

Thames-side Villages

BUT compact and picturesque as is the village of Corringham, it is nothing to be compared with Fobbing, which lies only half-a-mile further east. Here is a larger church, with a lofty stone steeple, a well-known beacon from Sea Reach, standing on the most commanding point of the promontory. To reach it the road first drops down into a little valley and crosses a tiny brook, then clambers up a short, steep hill on the other side, at the top of which one cannot fail to stop and notice a quaintly built old inn, 'The Bull,' which seems to bid us a kindly welcome. Past the church, the lane, bordered by small weather-timbered cottages and red-tiled roofs descends into the marshes and there ends. . . . A narrow tidal creek washes the base of the slopes, and at its head stands a small quay, with a plaster house of many corners and gables, once probably an inn, now much decayed. A black wooden warehouse, on piles, slants ominously over the water; a many-coloured barge, with tawny sails, brailed up and stowed, lies at anchor in the channel; above them all soars the grey-worn masonry of the church tower. Add a number of tall trees that shade the brightly-flowered cottage gardens, dipping down the hill, and you have the picture as complete as I can delineate it. . . . We must not forget that once in its existence this insignificant village figured largely in English history. Here it was that Jack Straw (the assumed name of an unknown priest) raised the standard of the great social revolt in the fourteenth century. The rising, as is well known, was in the end suppressed—not before the natives of the county had fought two stubborn engagements at Billericay.

PERCY CLARK, *Essex Review*, 1902.

A Vanished Village

UPON a fertile spot of land
Does Plaistow, thriving Plaistow, stand;
The sea, which whilome rowl'd his flood,
And hither brought the fatt'ning mud,
Has left a richness in the soil,
That well rewards the peasants' toil,
One side the level marshes sees,
And all is interspers'd with trees.

From hence the silver Thames appears,
And the wing'd vessels which he bears;

In which the vast supplies of trade
To fam'd Augusta are convey'd,
A pleasing sight to see them ride,
With sails unfurl'd, with wind and tide!

* * * *

But wand'ring muse, no flights pursue,
Keep Plaistow always in thy view.
Grand ships may sail where'er they please,
But little vessels coast the seas.
A lofty genius may explore
New regions, but keep thou the shore
Within thy ken; those dangers shun,
On which the bold and foolish run.

You that a soft retirement chuse,
And to a point contract your views,
May here enjoy a safe retreat
From pomp, and ev'rything that's great,
Here are you free from noise and strife,
And all those carking cares of life
That plague the town; from jilting jade,
From nauseous fops, and bites in trade.

London Mag., January 1734.

LEIGH STRAND—which was the older and more proper name of the High Street—was an amazing lesson in mediæval domestic architecture. Its southern side was built on the sea shore, and high water set the back yards and out-houses awash. The conformation of the shore settled, roughly, the contour of the street on this side, with violent modifications occasioned by the fact that no two houses were of the same size, nor had a common line of frontage; the contour of the north side was settled on the principle of complete disagreement with that of the south.

Our Villages The houses pushed their gables in every possible direction, an irresolute crowd; some interiors were attained by perilous ascent of brick steps, worn and broken, others by a precipitous flounder through a low doorway and down a doubtful stair. There was no brick house from end to end, and rain leaks in roofs and elsewhere were stopped with daubings of pitch, patches of which diversified every red roof in sight; for it would seem to be a principle that everything in Leigh, no matter what, must be repaired, when repair was needed, exactly as if it were a boat.

Arthur Morrison, *Cunning Murrell*, 1900.

Flora of the County

Our Flora THE alluvium and riverside flora, owing to the abundant streams and rivers of the county, are well and occasionally profusely represented. Amongst such plants may be named the white and yellow water lilies, the meadow rue, the greater spearwort, the purple and yellow loosestrifes, almost all the varieties of mints, the yellow and sweet flags, the willow herb, hemp agrimony, the common valerian, the teasle, the bulrush, the great flowering rush, etc.

The marine flora of Essex are numerous and representative. On the stretches of shingle and sand bordering the sea limit grow the horned poppy, sea rocket, sea kale and saltwort, together with various species of orache and sea spurge. The flora of the wide stretch of 'saltings' include golden and marsh samphires, thrift, sea lavenders, sea aster, sea blite, and scurvy grass; whilst waste ground and banks near the sea are well supplied with pepperworts, sea campion, sea lettuce, asparagus, sea wormwood, and wild celery, sea holly, etc.

Our Flora

Undoubtedly the most interesting plant of Essex is the true or Bardfield oxlip (*Primula elatior*). It is a beautiful primula, and ought not to be confounded with various hybrids between the cowslip and the primrose. This plant blooms freely, sometimes in extraordinary profusion, in the woods around Bardfield, Thaxted, and Saffron Walden; its habitat extends northward for some little distance into the adjoining counties of Suffolk, Cambridge and Hertford, but it occurs nowhere else throughout England. This delightful primula is confined to the boulder clay, and it is a highly remarkable fact that where it occurs it entirely replaces the primrose. There are three flowering plants said to be found nowhere else but in special localities in Essex. They are the sickle-leaved hare's ear (*Bupleurum falcatum*), which is abundant in parts of the Ongar district, particularly at Norton Mandeville: the red flowering Fyfield pea (*Lathyrus tuberosus*) found only in cornfields at Fyfield, to the north of Ongar; and a variety of the bedstraw (*Galium Vaillentii*) termed small-fruited goose grass, discovered in 1844, and which has now spread over a wide district round Saffron Walden, particularly in potato fields.

J. C. Cox, *Essex* (Little Guides).

OUR STREAMS, HILLS AND OYSTERS

THIS country is nearly on all sides encompassed by water. . . . Rivers and numerous running streams enliven and fertilize it . . . Brooks and rivulets add to the beauty and freshness of almost every parish in the county.

THOMAS WRIGHT, *History of Essex*, 1842.

Fools gaze at painted courts, to th' country let me go,
To climb the easy hill, then walk the valley low;
No gold-embossëd roofs to me are like the woods;
No bed is like the grass, no liquor like the floods.

At mighty Neptune's beck, thus ended they their song,
When as from Harwich all to Loving-land along,
Great claps and shouts were heard resounding to the shore,
Wherewith th' Essexian nymphs applaud their lovëd Stour.

MICHAEL DRAYTON, *Polyolbion*.

The great glory of Maldon is its river. The Chelmer and Blackwater unite at Maldon and have formed the fine estuary which is still known by the name of the Blackwater, the Idumania of Ptolemy. The tide flows up to Beeleigh Mill, past Beeleigh Abbey in the bed of the Chelmer.

EDWARD A. FITCH, *Maldon and the Blackwater*.

THE Muse now over Thames makes forth,
Upon her progress to the North,
From Canvey with a full career,
She up against the stream doth bear ;
Where Waltham Forest's pride exprest,
She points directly to the East,
And shows how all those Rivers strain
Through Essex to the German Main.

* * * *

When Hatfield taking heart, where late she sadly stood,
Sends little Roding forth, her best-beloved Flood ;
Which from her crystal fount, as to enlarge her fame,
To many a village lends her dear and noble name,
Which as she wand'reth on, through Waltham holds her way,
With goodly oaken wreaths which makes her wondrous gay ;
But making at the last into the wat'ry marsh,
Where though the blady grass unwholesome be and harsh,
Those wreaths away she casts, which bounteous Waltham gave,
With bulrush, flags and reed to make her wondrous brave,
And herself's strength divides to sundry lesser streams,
So wantoning she falls into her sovereign Thames.
From whose vast beechy banks a rumour straight resounds,
Which quickly ran itself through the Essexian grounds,
That Crouch amongst the rest, a River's name should seek,
As scorning any more the nickname of a Creek,

Streams and Rivers

Well furnished with a stream, that from the fill to
fall,
Wants nothing that a flood should be adorned with-
all.
Choice Chelmer comes along, a Nymph most
neatly clear,
Which well-near through the midst doth cut the
wealthy sheere.
By Dunmow gliding down to Chelmsford holds
her chase,
To which she gives the name, which as she doth
embrace
Clear Can comes tripping in, and doth with
Chelmer close :
With whose supply (though small as yet) she
greater grows.
She for old Maldon makes, where in her passing by,
She to remembrance calls that Roman colony.
When Chelmer scarce arrives in her most wish'd
bay,
But Blackwater comes in, through many a crooked
way,
Which Pant was called of yore ; but that, by Time
exiled,
She Freshwell after hight, then Blackwater in-
styled.
But Colne, which frankly lends fair Colchester her
name
(On all the Essexian shore, the Town of greatest
fame),
Perceiving how they still in courtship did contend,
Quoth she, wherefore the time thus idly do you
spend ?
What is there nothing here that you esteem of
worth,
That our big-bellied sea or our rich land brings
forth ?
Think you our Oysters here unworthy of your
praise ?

Pure Walfleet, which do still the daintiest palates please:
The Cizic shells, or those on the Lucrinian coast;
Or Cheese, which our fat soil to every quarter sends,
Whose tack the hungry clown and plow-man so commends.
If you esteem not these, as things above the ground,
Look under, where the urns of ancient times are found:
The Roman Emp'rours' coins, oft digg'd out of the dust,
And warlike weapons, now consum'd with cank'ring rust.
The huge and mossy bones of mighty fearful men,
To tell the world's full strength what creatures lived then,
When in her height of youth the lusty fruitful earth
Brought forth her big-limbed brood, even giants in their birth.

MICHAEL DRAYTON, *Polyolbion*, 1622.

The Roding

THE road from Chipping Ongar for its entire length runs in close contiguity to the river Roding, and in not a few places the views upon this pretty little stream are attractive, particularly between Chigwell and Chigwell Lane Station, where from the bridge the stream appears fringed with willow trees of considerable growth, and with its banks edged with a tangle of rushes and reeds.

C. R. B. BARRETT,
Essex: Highways, Byways and Waterways, 1892.

The Roding Valley

TWILIGHT already stealing over the landscape shades yonder sleeping cornfield, whence the merry reapers have this day borne away the last sheaf. A party of gleaners have since gathered up the precious fragments. Now all are gone : the harvest moon is up. A low mist rising from the river floats in the valley. There is a gentle stirring amongst the leaves of the tall elm that shades our roof. All besides is still.

JANE TAYLOR, *Contributions of Q. Q.*, 1824.

On the Stour

AS we glided on, past the loosestrife and the lilies,
The skies were blue above the winding Stour,
And though we knew the world might say that we were sillies,
For both that day held life's most blissful hour.

Then we neither knew what the purple flower portended
The winds of strife approaching her and me.
Till all too soon we found—our little voyage ended—
The longer one we planned was not to be.

The world is wide and sad, the waking world is weary,
The lodestar of my youth is far away ;
But though beneath the sun I never meet my dearie,
We often meet when night replaces day.

When all the world is still, and all the stars are gleaming
Their brightest in the firmament above ;

Rarely do I dream of their radiance : in my dreaming
I am still upon the river with my love.

What though Fate may flout us, what though we be sillies,
We are conscious yet of life's most blissful hour,
As we drift along past the loosestrife and the lilies,
While skies are blue above the winding Stour.

W. H. Harwood, (1910).

The Roothings

To all except hunting men, the large district of Essex now known as 'the Roothings' but formerly as 'the Rodings' is a veritable *terra incognita*. The eight (formerly nine) small parishes composing the district take their common name from the river Roding which flows through their midst. They are Abbess Roothing, Aythorpe Roothing, Beauchamp, Berners and High Roothing, Leaden Roothing, Margaret, White and Morell Roothing. The last is now incorporated with White Roothing. As old Norden, writing in 1594, says quaintly :—'The Roding first appeareth nere Takely, whence as she passeth she greeteth her nine daughters, all the Rodings.' All are thinly populated and purely rural. Their combined population amounted at the last census to 1885 souls, an average of 102 persons to the square mile, against an average of 704 to the square mile for the whole county. The Roothings lie on the way to nowhere in particular. They are neither intersected nor approached by any important main road; they contain no ancient earthwork, no picturesque ruin, no large church, not even a single monumental brass, and no residence of greater consequence than a large farmhouse or country parsonage. No district so near London (and the nearest portion of the Roothings lies within twenty-five miles of St. Paul's) is so little known.

MILLER CHRISTY, *Essex Review*, 1903.

Danbury Hill

FIVE miles east of Chelmsford, half way between that town and the ancient borough of Maldon, famous in Saxon annals, is a range of hills rising to a height of at least six hundred feet above the sea. On the south-east crest of this ridge stands the church and village of Danbury, the centre of this rural district. It would be hard to find a lovelier situation. The old roofs creep up the hillside and cluster round the still older church with the lofty spire which has been for centuries a beacon to the weary wanderer by land and to the storm-tossed wanderer at sea. Tall lime-trees grow up to the church doors; majestic wych-elms bend their graceful boughs over the grassy mounds where once the standard of the Black Raven flew. From these heights you can look down upon the ocean, across which the Norsemen sailed, and taste the salt of the sea breezes. Turn where you will a noble prospect meets the eye. Eastward the broad estuary of the Blackwater lies before you with white sails dotted over its blue surface, and churches and hamlets rising from its high banks. Southward, you look across the valley of the Crouch river and the Laindon Hills to the silver streak of the Thames and the far shores of Kent. All around you stretch beautiful commons with their wealth of colour and far-reaching views.

JULIA CARTWRIGHT,
'A Corner of Essex,' *National Review*, 1892.

Laindon Hills

A CARRIAGE was provided for us at Tilbury, and in the course of two hours reached the summit of Langdon Hill. Here I was gratified with the most delightful prospect my eyes ever beheld. Lady Tracy (of Billericay) caused the carriage to stop at certain intervals, that her daughter and I might be indulged with a full enjoyment of it; while she, to whom it was familiar, pointed out to us the most material objects. The country before us formed a beautiful enclosed valley, bounded towards the west and south-west by the distant hills of Highgate and Hampstead, and the Surrey hills, within which wide circuit appeared the great emporium of Europe, the city of London; thence I could trace the beautiful meanderings of the Thames, and the quantities of shipping passing and repassing. I saw the village of Tilbury below, and Gravesend, with the chalk cliffs of Kent, and the country rising like a vast amphitheatre from the marshes. Turning towards the east we discovered the conjunction of the Thames with the Medway, and the view was terminated by the blue tints of the salt sea, where it opens into the mouth of the British Channel.

JOSEPH STRUTT, *Queenhoo Hall*, 1808.

A PICTURESQUE range of hills in the south east part of Essex begins at Canewdon, runs round to Rayleigh in a rough semicircle, and then turns on to South Benfleet, where it ends. There are several steep roads down from Rayleigh to the plain on the west, one of them at Thundersley and the farthest at Bread and Cheese Hill, South Benfleet. A curious name this Bread and Cheese Hill; it is supposed by some people to have obtained its name from Wat Tyler's rebellion, which began in Essex at Fobbing, a village not very far off. The notion is this: the rebels hated the Flemings living in England, and when they caught a man whom they thought to be a Fleming, they made him say 'Bread and Cheese.' If he could not do this properly, they killed him. Thus they came to be called Bread and Cheese men. Now, when the rebels retreated before the King's men, they occupied all the high and wooded ground, and probably this range of hills. It is certain that there was a severe fight not far off, namely at Billericay [This is a true Essex shibboleth—pronounced Bill'ricky]. Anyhow, the steep hill down which the road near Jarvis Hall descends has been called Bread and Cheese Hill time out of mind.

W. E. HEYGATE, *An Old Parson's Tales*, 1892.

A Road in 1767

OF all the cursed roads that ever disgraced this kingdom in the very ages of barbarism, none ever equalled that from Billericay to the 'King's Head' at Tilbury. It is for twelve miles so narrow that a mouse cannot pass by any wagon, . . . the ruts are of an incredible depth except at a few places, and to add to all the infamous circumstances which occur to plague a traveller, I must not forget eternally meeting with chalk wagons, themselves frequently stuck fast until a collection of them are in the same situation, so that twenty or thirty horses may be tacked to each to draw them out, one by one.

ARTHUR YOUNG,
Tour through the Southern Counties, 1757.

AT one time the Essex roads, besides being sometimes 'almost impassable' were very dangerous, by reason of the numbers of highwaymen and deer-stealers who haunted the great forests, from the thick shelter of which it was extremely difficult to dislodge them. Epping (or Waltham) Forest held the worst offenders. In the fourteenth century a gang known as the Black Gang encamped near Waltham and took toll of the people going to the abbey, till the monks enclosed that part of the forest and drove them out. No traveller between Waltham and London in those days was ever safe. The road from that time onward was infested by gang after gang of robbers, who were protected from justice in the recesses of the wood. The most famous of these bands was formed in the later seventeenth century and largely composed of discharged soldiery. . . . An Act of 1692 proclaimed martial law against them, because 'the highways were more infested with thieves and robbers than formerly,' but though their numbers were thinned it was impossible to disperse the gangs altogether, and even at the end of the eighteenth century Epping Forest was still a source of danger to the community. It is alleged that farmers at that period had to return from Colchester market in companies, fearing robbery if they journeyed alone.

Roads and Inns

MISS NORA MACMUNN,
Victoria History of Essex (1907).

Inns on the Road

A CENTURY ago some forty coaches a day, besides humbler public vehicles, are said to have plied on the Essex trunk-road out of London; then its 'thoroughfare towns' would have no lack of custom for the 'White Hart' of

Brentwood, the 'Saracen's Head' of Chelmsford, and the 'Cups' of Colchester, where at any hour kings or queens might call for refreshment, as George III's bride did at a Romford coffee-house that still treasures the memory.

A. R. Hope Moncrieff, *Essex*.

Signboards and Inns

PROBABLY no better idea can now be obtained in Essex of an old-fashioned thoroughfare than in the broad High Street at Epping. From one point no less than ten sign-boards may be seen, all swinging over the pavement in the ancient style. Only one, however, the White Lion is pictorial. The number of inns in Grays is also large. It has been stated in print that, for its size, it contains more than any other town in England. In the narrow Tindal Street at Chelmsford the sign-boards still swing across the street in the old style and are hung upon the old supports. The best example is that of the Spotted Dog. Witham has many inns, nearly all of which have their sign-boards hanging over the pavement. Colchester has hardly such a thing as a projecting sign-board, let alone pictorial signs. Castle Hedingham, for its size, probably has more pictorial signs than any other Essex town—the Bell, the Crown, the Three Crowns, and the Rising Sun, being all represented. Except the sign-iron of the Six Bells, Dunmow contains but little of sign-board interest. The only pictorial sign in Ongar is that of the Cock. In the High Street, Romford, are many very old inns, but their signs are all script. At Leigh there are many inns, the most ancient of which are the Crown, and the Hambro' Merchants' Arms, though the George was originally the most important.

Miller Christy, *Trade Signs of Essex*, 1887.

Vale of Dedham

THE man who could faithfully depict the beauties of the Vale of Dedham had little cause to regret that his range was limited or to long for a wider one. Words cannot convey the charm of this lovely vale. Its beauty is too subtle to be grasped in detail, too various to be described in general terms. Just now as I lean against a field gate beside the Flatford road, it is full of lights and shades and overhung by slowly drifting clouds. Where the shadows lurk the outlines of the trees and homesteads are hardly definable ; even the borders of the fields and pastures are scarcely perceptible ; but where the sunlight falls every waterside willow and poplar, every cottage and hedgerow, and farmstead stands out clear and beautiful, each a picture in itself. Subject to the clouds' drift, the swathes of light and shade steal in quick succession through the vale, and presently the tall square tower of Dedham Church — so conspicuous a feature of Constable's picture of the vale — reveals itself amid a grove of trees. Around the church lies the village which gives its name to the vale, and beyond it and the slow-flowing river are the Essex cornfields. Go into the National Gallery and look at Constable's 'Cornfield,' and you will see one of these Essex fields. In the foreground of the picture is a winding lane, beyond which the yellow corn is bathed in sunlight. Through an open gateway you see the corn-stalks bowing before the wind. Beyond the field is Dedham Church, which the artist could seldom keep out of his pictures of his homeland. Beside the lane is a brook into which the brambles dip their bending briars, arching from banks where wave the white umbels of wild parsleys. Along the rough wagon track a dog drives a flock of sheep, while their young shepherd lies down to drink of the waters of the brook.

WILLIAM A. DUTT,
Highways and Byways in East Anglia, 1901.

Sunset at Southend

AS one walks down the High Street of that popular watering-place, the pier lies directly in front, running out a mile and a quarter to sea on its myriad slender feet, like a gigantic centipede. To the left, with lips drooped to the water's edge, the Old Town straggles away seaward, a broken line of picturesque irregular buildings—some cheerful red, others warm yellow, and a few cool grey—reminding one not a little of some quaint French or Belgian port, blinking in the morning sunshine.

To the right are the shady shrubberies and wooded slopes of the West Cliff. Sunny little Southend-on-Salt-Water may be unable to show such a sea as one found at big, boastful Brighton, but it is a green and homelike spot, and not mere brick and mortar by the briny. Here are no long lines of stuccoed mansions, and staring straight parades, but grass, sweet and springy, as on a Surrey common, and sloping flower-strewn heights that run down waterward, like a happy child that hastens with outstretched arms towards the sea. And oh! such skies! such cloud-pomp and pageantry, and above all such sunrises and sunsets! Such dance and sparkle of moving water when the tide is in; and more beautiful still, when the tide is out, such play of light and shadow, such wonderful wealth of colour on the marshy flats—here a patch of royal purple or opalescent green, here a rose-grey or pearly pink, with little shining pools that change from blue to silver, and from silver to blue, with the passing of every cloud.

COULSON KERNAHAN, *Captain Shannon*, 1897.

Best Wallfleets

SOME part of the sea shore of Essex yealdeth the beste oysters in England, which are called Walflete oysters ; so called of a place in the sea between St Peter's Chappell and Crowche Creeke, where upon the verie shore was erected a wall for the preservation of the lande. And all the seashore which beateth on that wall is called the Walfleet. It is a little full oyster with a verie greene fynn, and like unto this in quantitie and qualitie are none in this lande.

JOHN NORDEN, *Description of Essex*.

THE old luxurious Romans vaunts did make
Of gustful oysters took in Lucrine Lake,
Your Essex better hath, and such perchance
As tempted Cæsar first to pass from France.

SIR ASTON COCKAIN, 1669.

The Song of the Oyster

THOUGH scaly foes on every side abound,
The cool, tenacious oyster holds his ground:
Impassive, calm, in temper unexcelled,
He shuts his mouth unless he is compelled,
And when he opens, as sometimes he should,
What he imparts is for the public good,
Nothing superfluous to vex or waste,
But all agreeable and in perfect taste.

Chorus—

Lords and ladies, knights and squires,
Holy abbots, priests and friars,
Aldermen and bailiffs too,
Councillors in robes of blue,
When you come to think about it,
Think about it,
Think about it,
Isn't THIS a pattern which might do for you?

Though men may rudely drag him from his shell,
And probe and prod and pepper him as well,
And sour his mild existence—yet what then?
To live for some brief space in mouths of men
Is fame, and this fulfils the oyster's mission:
To please and satisfy is his ambition;
And though not proud, his gentle heart will flutter
To know he's worthy of his bread and butter!

Chorus—

Lords and ladies, knights and squires, etc.

W. GURNEY BENHAM (1908).

OUR FOREST

Alwaies especiallie and above all theire other fforests prized and esteemed by the Kinges Majestie and his said noble progenitors the Kinges and Queenes of this Realme of England, as well for his and theire own pleasure, disport and recreation from those pressing cares for the publique weale and safetie which are inseparablie incident to theire kinglie office, as for the interteynment of foreyne Princes and Embassadors, thereby to show unto them the magnificence of the Kinges and Queenes of this Realme.

Exchequer Bills of Charles I.

Lo! I will get me to the woods and try
If I my woodcraft have forgotten quite.

William Morris, *Earthly Paradise.*

The Forest was thrown open to the Public by Queen Victoria at High Beech, 6th May, 1882, and thus by the exertions and at the sole cost of the Corporation of London, a district originally taken from the ancient folkland for the exclusive use of the Sovereigns was, after many centuries, dedicated by the hands of their successor to the use and enjoyment of her subjects.

W. R. Fisher, *Forest of Essex*, 1888.

Gipsies

EPPING FOREST . . . the loveliest forest in the world! not equal to what it was, but still the loveliest forest in the world, and the pleasantest, especially in summer; for then it is thronged with grand company, and the nightingales, and cuckoos, and Romany chals and chies [gipsy lads and lasses]. As for Romany-chals there is not such a place for them in the whole world as the Forest. Them that wants to see Romany-chals should go to the Forest, especially to the Bald-faced Hind on the hill above Fairlop, on the day of Fairlop Fair. It is their trysting-place, as you would say, and there they musters from all parts of England, and there they whoops, dances and plays; keeping some order, nevertheless, because the Rye of all the Romans is in the house, seated behind the door.

Our Forest

GEORGE BORROW, *Romano Lavo Lil*, 1905.

I LOVE the Forest and its airy bounds,
Where friendly Campbell takes his daily rounds.

* * * *

I love to see the Beech Hill mounting high,
The brook without a bridge, and nearly dry.
There's Buckhurst Hill, a place of furze and clouds
Which evening in a golden blaze enshrouds.

I loved the forest walks and beechen woods,
Where pleasant Stockdale showed me far away
Wild Enfield Chase and pleasant Edmonton.
While giant London, known to all the world,
Was nothing but a guess among the trees,
Though only half a day from where we stood.
Such is ambition! only great at home
And hardly known to quiet and repose.

JOHN CLARE (1837).

THE forest in winter, the forest in spring, in summer, and in autumn—which is finest? Indeed, I do not know. . . . Truly the forest is very magnificent in summer, when under the trees the brilliant light is held in check by the thick leafage. But for those who can see, there is a greater magnificence in late autumn. For then the woods lie over the hills in a broken tumult of mellow colour. All shades—brilliant yellow, full browns, sober crimsons, and heavy olives—mingle in a strange harmony, as sober and as quiet as it is rich. But then the winter brings beauties of its own. When the hoar-frost makes the woods a world of white lace, when the ground is like granite and the clear air is sharp and tingling on the face, you may stand in Monk Wood, or you may overlook the forest from Loughton Camp, and see that natural beauty is no mere matter of green leaves and golden sunlight. . . . And for the remaining season, have not a hundred poets sung of spring in the woods? When the sap rises over the six thousand acres of Epping Forest here is spring indeed, spring as no words can paint it. But for that—go and see.

ARTHUR MORRISON, *The Traveller*, July 1901.

IN the seasons when the forest is least frequented it is also the most beautiful. In spring the different greens of the various trees are wonderfully striking, from a point such as High Beech where a wide stretch of woodland can be seen.

Even when the skies are dark with gathering snow a wonderful picture is presented by the wooded ridges, the nearer ones blended into a mass of sepia contrasting with the opal blue of the more distant. But the forest in autumn is most wonderful of all, when the russet and gold of the trees are bathed in the calm sunshine of Indian summer; the hillsides are clothed with purple heather, or with glowing masses of copper-coloured bracken; and the vivid green grass is sprinkled with fallen leaves of the brightest scarlet.

It is amid such surroundings as these that we come upon the famous Ambresbury Banks, which tradition points out as the scene of the struggle between Boadicea and Suetonius, but where at all events is a camp of very early origin. The ancient earthworks are still quite distinct, although imperfect and much obscured by trees. Standing upon the top of the rampart, one may hear the cooing of the wood-pigeons, watch the rabbits scampering in and out of their warrens, or perhaps catch a glimpse of the fallow deer whose progenitors were brought here by the countrymen of Suetonius. . . .

It is the virgin loveliness of Monk's Wood and Ambresbury Banks that makes a modern writer of refined taste call even the New Forest commonplace in comparison. Chingford must be passed over by the traveller who wishes to feel and retain the impression of Epping Forest as a romantic solitude. Let him begin among the trees on the higher ground until the hush of evening falls, and depart eastward into the quiet valley of the Roding as the white mists rise in the darkening hollows under the pale gleam of the moonrise.

REGINALD A. BECKETT, *Romantic Essex*, 1901.

Spring and Autumn

OF the thousands of Londoners who refresh themselves by a visit to our groves, comparatively few do so at the two periods of the year when they are most beautiful—early May and late October. To the tree-lover I strongly recommend the former month. It is then, when the first burst of spring takes place, that the distinguishing characteristics, and especially the *colours* of each tree, can be best seen. A few weeks later the yellow of the young oak foliage, the grey-green of the birches and the burnished light-reflecting quality of the beeches, are merged in one uniform dark green, lovely in its varied shapes and play of light and deep shadow, but monotonous as to colour. The blackthorn in April, the hawthorn in May, a month later the crab, and sheets of the water-violet and water-ranunculus, supply the masses of white without which no group either of flowers or trees is complete. Again in the 'fall,' when our glades are almost solitudes, who can measure the glories of the beech groves when they put on their first autumn touches of brown and gold, contrasting with the dark green of the more persistent oak, and with the saffron yellow of the birch and maple? No leaf-colouring can be found to surpass these in brilliance.

EDWARD NORTH BUXTON, *Epping Forest*, 1905.

September in the Forest

THROUGH the long weeks of summer, day
by day
Came London forth on the bleached sward
to play;
But now the town has claimed its own again.
The patient grass, tired with the summer heat
And with the passing of ten thousand feet,
Lies all deserted, waiting for the rain.

No more are heard the childrens' voices shrill,
The laughter, shouts, and music all are still;

Only the wistful robin's autumn song
Among the sombre trees in rusty green,
Breaks silence where for many a day has been
The alien presence of a noisy throng.

Soon the glad rain will cleanse the weary land,
The early frost will lay its magic hand
On every bush and tree, and there shall leap
Forth one last flame of crimson, russet, gold,
To clothe the woods in glories manifold
Before they sink into their winter's sleep.

E. F. HOWARD, 1901.

WHEN I was a boy and young man I knew the Forest yard by yard from Wanstead to the Theydons and from Hale End to the Fairlop Oak. In those days it had no worse foes than the gravel stealer and the rolling fence-maker, and was always interesting and often very beautiful. The special character of it was derived from the fact that by far the greater part was a wood of hornbeams, a tree not common save in Essex and Herts. It was certainly the biggest hornbeam wood in these islands, and I suppose in the world. The said hornbeams were all pollards, being shrouded every four or six years, and were interspersed in many places with holly thickets. Nothing could be more interesting and romantic than the effect of the long poles of the hornbeams rising from the trunks and seen against the mass of the wood behind. It has a peculiar charm of its own not to be found in any other forest.

WILLIAM MORRIS, *Life*, 1901.

THERE he formed his intense love of nature and his keen eye for all sorts of woodland life. He never ceased to love Epping Forest and to uphold the scenery of his native county as beautifully and characteristically English.

 The dense hornbeam thickets, which even in bright weather have something of solemnity and mystery in their deep shade, and which are hardly found elsewhere in England, reappear again and again in his poetry and his prose romances.

J. W. MACAIL, *Life of Morris*, 1901.

A Glade in the Forest

SO he came to where the land was level, and there were many trees, as oak and ash, and sweet-chestnut and wych-elm, and hornbeam and quicken-tree, not growing in a close wood or tangled thicket, but set as though in order on the flowery greensward, even as it might be in a great king's park. So came he to a big bird-cherry, whereof many boughs hung low down, laden with fruit. . . . And the scent of that fair land came up to him like the odour of one great nosegay.

WILLIAM MORRIS,
The Wood beyond the World, 1895.

THERE is one fault, and only one, which can be alleged against my forest. It is sometimes undoubtedly wet under foot. The soil is clay and the water lies in little pools. One cannot deny the charge. This day, fortunately, it was dry; there had been sunshine for nearly a week, a most wonderful thing for this rain-plagued climate of England. We could walk anywhere; through the narrow lanes arched over with the tender foliage of the spring, among the old trunks where there were no lanes at all, and over the broad stretches of turf which once had been our playground, our racecourse, our theatre.

'This is the forest,' said Gertrude, looking round her, 'which made Allen what he is. . . . In this place one might dream away a lifetime. Of course Allen became a poet.'

'The forest is not always so gracious,' I said. 'Sometimes it is wet and muddy, sometimes in cloudy weather it loses its colour, and in cold east winds it loses its perfume.'

'A forest is like the sea,' said Gertrude. 'Its moods are many; they are never quite the same; and one never tires of it, and one is always tempted to say something about it—something which shall be new, a thing never said before. Like the sea it satisfies; it is sympathetic; it responds to every thought. . . .'

The next day and the day after, and the day after that, we showed our guests all our beautiful places; we drove about through leafy lanes and past picturesque cottages standing in the midst of flowers; we went to the quiet little town of Abridge, on the river Roding, standing in a circle as if it had once been within a round wall; we showed them the wild parts of Epping Forest and Copped Hall Park, and the burial place among the quiet trees of Harold and his brothers; we took them to Chigwell, with its great trees and solemn churchyard, and to old Chingford Church, falling slowly and sadly to pieces, with shattered windows and bending roof and bare interior, and quiet old place of graves, which looks out upon the broad valley of the Lea. Everywhere there were trees with sunshine, flowers and the singing of birds and a sweet calm.

'My dear,' said Gertrude, 'this is the true birthplace of a poet.'

'Yet at the West End you know nothing of it.'

'I thought that Epping and all about it was given over to the mob who drink beer and break branches and shout,' she said.

'Only a little of the forest. Beyond High Beech you have solitude and quiet. At Hainault we are nearly always left in peace. And the quiet lanes beyond are never visited.'

WALTER BESANT, *All in a Garden Fair*, 1883.

Epping Forest

WOODS and coppices by tempest lashed;
Pollard shockheads glaring in the rain;
Jet-black underwood with crimson splashed,
Rich November, one wet crimson stain!

Turf that whispered moistly to the tread;
Bursts of laughter from the shuffled leaves;
Pools of light in distant arbours spread;
Depths of darkness under forest eaves.

High above the wind the clouds at rest
Emptied every vat and steeply hurled
Reservoirs and floods; the wild nor'-west
Raked the downpour ere it reached the world;

Part in wanton sport and part in ire,
Flights of rain on ruddy foliage rang:
Woven showers like sheets of silver fire
Streamed; and all the forest rocked and sang.

JOHN DAVIDSON, *Holiday and Other Poems*, 1906.

Of the Same

FROM Epping Street where half a score
Inviting hostels lie between
The upper forest and the lower,
The bounds and metes of that demesne
That once from Waltham surged in green

Luxuriance to the northern tide,
The lover of the fall's serene,
Miraculous renascence, hied
By turnpike, woodland path and forest ride.

A purple haze that scarce could keep
Diaphanous consistence spread
Above the ridged perspective deep
Of Epping Forest ; overhead,
With arabesque of shining thread
As manifold as jewelled dyes,
In varied beauty interwed,
A snowy vapour damaskwise
Endued the tenderest of turquoise skies.

Ripples of cloudlike silver strands
Escaloped by continual surge,
The seaboard of fantastic lands,
Defined the welkin's orient verge :
He heard afar the airy dirge
Of breaking billows, saw the foam
In heaven's mantle, spindrift scourge
The zenith, and their shadows roam
Across the woods like coveys flying home.

A herd of clouds with fleeces rent
Flocked in the west ; an aigret plumed
The low-hung northern firmament ;
But in the south a shadow loomed
Like chaos out of eld exhumed
To re-engulf the world long lost
In time ; and yet the darkness bloomed
With sprays of bronze-like briars tossed,
With hidden flower and fruit of flame embossed.

He heard the woodman's fateful strokes
In Epping Thicket, blow on blow,
Where spaciously the loftiest oaks
In all the forest precincts grow.

The rose, the bramble and the sloe
Muffled the holly, hid the thorn ;
And berries blushed with diverse glow
Of gradual colour like the morn,
Whose changing hues the ravished east adorn.

In many a dome of russet green,
Without a centre shaft to draw,
The branches round it, might be seen,
One more with tender-hearted awe,
The burning bush religion saw—
The nightshade's coral hanging free,
The scarlet hip, the crimson haw,
The swarthy bramble lovingly
Enwreathed as in a myriad-minded tree.

The bramble leaves, with iron mould
Distained, like metal foliage glanced ;
The fluted beech, in ruddy gold
Accoutred bravely, countenanced
The yellow thorn, whose hue enhanced
In turn the heather's rusty ore ;
The bracken, faded all, advanced
Along the forest's pillared floor—
A tawny tide upon an emerald shore.

But eager frosts that braise and brand
Autumnal foliage still delayed ;
Green was the forest, green the land,
A fibrous sward, a toothsome blade ;
The cow-bells rang in every glade
Their quaint memorial refrain,
A ghostly sound by change unlaid ;
The year stood still ; and summer, fain
As in her prime, usurped the world again.

The chrysosperm in sunbeams pent
A largesse squandered. Rich as light
Of rainbow brede, the forest scent ;
And subtler, keener than the white

Aroma of the stars at night
That maddens lovers wandering late
Betrothed in destiny's despite ;
As searching as the importunate
And supersensuous ether uncreate.

A doe stepped forth and pried about
With wondering look and watchful ear,
Then vanished. Venturous birds burst out
As in the heydey of the year
With summer song in snatches, clear
As water dropping in a well ;
Harmonious from a turret near
Replied a silvery vesper-bell ;
The braided light grew golden ; evening fell.

In Highbeech Holt, a place alone,
A wonder of the world, antique
Protected beeches straightly grown,
Or pollarded of yore and meek
Transmuters of the shapeless freak
The iron wrought throughout the years
To symmetry, that all things seek
For ever, they, the verderer's
Most cherished vert in all his marks and meres,

Upon a forest fabric stood
Three—piles of leaves and fruitful mast,
That carpeted the upland wood
And crypts and bowers, obscure and vast
In the close twilight waning fast :
Some scumbled moss, with here and there
A stroke of scanty herbage, cast
A chord of green, remarked and rare
Among the russet spreading everywhere.

All still and stately ancient trees,
With stem erect and ample bole,

Maintained their native majesties
In leafy robe and verdant stole
Invested, green from fork to poll;
Old, gnarled and thundersmitten, some
Uncouthly grew, the sylvan soul
By brutal accident become
A tortured wraith in hideous anguish dumb.

The saplings flourished straight and tall
Like living palisades a-row,
Their lance-like stems in vertical
And rhythmic parallels below;
Above like crayon lines that flow
Obliquely through each other, swart
Immingled boughs in writhen throe
A cross-hatched canopy athwart
The precinct flung and roofed the arboured court.

A silence like the dead of night
The ebon-pillared emerald walls
Immured; a dusky latticed light
Fulfilled the high-groined cloisters, halls,
Occult recesses, wildwood stalls
In glimmering chancel aisles arrayed;
And violet beams at intervals,
Illumed the forest-girdled glade
Through rents and loopholes in the beechen shade.

With hue and form so diverse stored,
Beauty and wonder, vaulted space
By fantasy alone explored,
The solitude and rich embrace
Soul-clasping of that silent place
So sphered his vision, steeped his brain
In dreams, that he beheld no trace
Of mundane things, nor hint nor stain
Of twilight or of night, until again

He reached the city. Then and there
A potent urban spell subdued
The forest's, for the sorcerer
Of sorcerers is multitude. . . .

JOHN DAVIDSON, From 'Liverpool Street Station,' *Fleet Street and other Poems*, 1909.

CHIGWELL, my dear fellow, is the greatest place in the world. Name your day for going. Such a delicious old inn opposite the churchyard—such a lovely ride—such beautiful forest scenery—such an out-of-the-way rural place—such a sexton! I say again, name your day.

CHARLES DICKENS, *Letter to John Forster*, 1872.

The King's Head, Chigwell

IN the year 1775 there stood upon the borders of Epping Forest, at a distance of about twelve miles from London, a house of public entertainment called the 'Maypole.' The Maypole was an old building, with more gable ends than a lazy man would care to count on a sunny day; huge zig-zag chimneys, out of which it seemed as though even smoke could not choose but come in more than naturally fantastic shapes, imparted to it in its tortuous progress; and vast stables, gloomy, ruinous, and empty. The place was said to have been built in the days of King Henry the Eighth, and there was a legend not only that Queen Elizabeth had slept there one night while on a hunting excursion—to wit, in a certain oak-panelled room with a big bay window—but that next morning, while standing on a mounting-block before the door with one foot in the stirrup, the virgin monarch had then and there boxed and cuffed an unlucky page for some neglect of duty. Whether these and many other stories of a like nature were true or untrue, the Maypole was really an old house, a very old house, perhaps as old as it claimed to be, and perhaps older, which will sometimes happen with houses of an uncertain, as with ladies of a certain age. The windows were old diamond-pane lattices, its floors were sunken and uneven, its ceilings blackened by the hand of time, and heavy with massive beams. Over the doorway was an ancient porch, quaintly and grotesquely carved, and here on summer evenings the more favoured customers smoked and drank—ay, and sang many a good song too, sometimes reposing on two grim-looking high-backed settles, which, like the twin dragons of some fairy tale, guarded the entrance to the mansion.

In the chimneys of the disused rooms swallows had built their nests for many a long year, and from earliest spring to latest autumn whole colonies of sparrows chirped and twittered in the eaves. There were more pigeons about the dreary stable yard and outbuildings than anybody but the landlord could reckon up. The wheeling and circling flights of runts, fantails, tumblers, and pouters were perhaps not quite consistent with the grave and sober character of the building, but the monotonous cooing, which never ceased to be raised by some among them all day long, suited it exactly, and seemed to lull it to rest. With its overhanging storeys, drowsy little panes of glass, and front bulging out and projecting over the pathway, the old house looked as if it were nodding in its sleep. The brick of which it was built had originally been a deep dark red, but had grown yellow and discoloured like an old man's skin ; the sturdy timbers had decayed like teeth ; and here and there the ivy, like a warm garment to comfort it in its age, wrapt its green leaves closely round the time-worn walls.

It was a hale and hearty age though still, and in the summer or autumn evenings, when the glow of the setting sun fell upon the oak and chestnut trees of the adjacent forest, the old house, partaking of its lustre, seemed their fit companion, and to have many good years of life in him yet.

CHARLES DICKENS, *Barnaby Rudge*, 1841.

A Grant from the King

THE forest of Epping and Hainault spreads over a great part of this country still. . . . Probably this forest of Epping has been a wild or forest ever since this island was inhabited, and may show us, in some parts of it, where enclosures and tillage have not broken in upon it, what the general face of this island was before the Romans landed in Britain.

The constitution of this forest is best seen, I mean as to the antiquity of it, by the pleasant grant of it from Edward the Confessor before the Norman Conquest to Randolph Peperking, one of his favourites, who was after called Peverell, and whose name remains still in several villages in this county; as particularly that of Hatfield Peverell, in the road from Chelmsford to Witham, which is supposed to be originally a park, which they called a field in those days; and Hartfield may be as much as to say, a park for deer, for the stags were in those days called harts ; so that this was neither more nor less than Randolph Peperking's Hartfield—that is to say, Ralph Peverell's deer-park. . . . Thus we have several towns, where any ancient parks have been placed, called by the name of Hatfield on that very account, as Hatfield Broad Oak in this county; Bishop's Hatfield in Hertfordshire, and others. But I return to King Edward's pleasant way, as I call it, of granting this forest to this Ralph Peperking, which I find in the ancient records, in the very words it was passed, as follows. Take my explanation of it for the sake of those that are not used to the ancient English:

'I Edward the King, have made ranger of my forest of Chelmsford hundred and Deering hundred, Ralph Peverell, for him and his heirs for ever; with both the red and fallow deer, hare and fox, otter and badger, wild fowl of all sorts, partridges and pheasants, timber and underwood, roots and tops; with power to preserve the Forest. And watch it against deer-stealers and others; with a right to keep hounds of all sorts, four greyhounds and six terriers, harriers and fox-hounds, and other hounds. And to this end I have registered this my grant in the Crown Rolls or books; to which Bishop Wolston has set his hand as a witness for anyone to read. Also signed by the King's brother (or, as some think, the Chancellor Sweyn, then Earl or Count of Essex). And by such other witnesses as he thought fit. Also by Howelin, the King's high steward, at whose request this grant was obtained.'

DANIEL DEFOE,
Tour through the Eastern Counties, (1722).

The Trees of the Forest

A PART only of the Essex Forest remains to recall the once great forest of the East Saxon Kingdom which had Lundentune for its port and ecclesiastical centre. . . .

Epping Forest is not a London County Council park, whose natural features are preserved with metalled roads and gravelled paths to make easy the way of recreators. It is what it claims to be —a forest: a strip of wild woodland, whose paths, but trodden tracks, lose themselves in a maze of wanderings, now amid the groves, now through heath and bracken fern, now through the moist beds of tiny rivulets, to discover pool and pond. Both hill and dale are clothed with pollarded hornbeam, centuries old. Upon the dry uplands flourish the beeches, the finest trees of the forest. Oaks are in a minority; giant trees but few: the oldest, the decaying Fairmead Oak, round whose mighty base have thronged thousands of sporting Londoners in the days of the famous Easter hunt. Rugged old crab-apple trees—favourites with the deer for their sour fruit—are here in goodly num-numbers. Blackthorn affords dense impenetrable brushwood and a sanctuary for the birds. . . . The half-day's journey which separated the ambitious city from 'the forest walks and beechen woods,' beloved of the poet Clare, is now reduced to one of little more than half an hour. From the high ground amid the woods the eye instinctively turns to where 'the city lies beneath its drift of smoke,' or sees at night 'in heaven the light of London flaring like a dreary dawn,' as Tennyson wrote, when living in the forest at High Beech. . . . In the forest to-day King Demos reigns supreme, and the former tyrannical restrictions by the kings of England are forgotten by those who enter it at will and wander where once to tread would have been a trespass.

PERCIVAL J. S. PERCEVAL, *London's Forest*, 1909.

The Broad Oak of Hatfield Forest

(*d.* 1858)

Our Forest

A MIGHTY growth! The county side
Lamented when the giant died,
For England loves her trees:
What misty legends round him cling,
How lavishly he once could fling,
His acorns to the breeze!

Who struck a thousand roots in fame,
Who gave the district half its name,
Will not be soon forgotten.
Last spring he show'd but one green bough,
The red leaves hang there yet—and now
His very props are rotten.

* * * *

Elate, the thunderbolt he braved,
For centuries his branches waved
A welcome to the blast;
From reign to reign he bore a spell,
No Forester had dared to fell,
What time has felled at last.

The Monarch wore a leafy crown,
And wolves, ere wolves were hunted down,
Found shelter in his gloom;
Unnumber'd squirrels frolick'd free,
Glad music fill'd the gallant tree
From stem to topmost bloom.

It's hard to say, 'twere vain to seek
When first he ventured forth, a meek
Petitioner for dew;
No Saxon spade disturbed his root,
The rabbit spared the tender shoot,
And valiantly he grew,

And show'd some inches from the ground
When Saint Augustine came and found
    Us very proper Vandals :
Then nymphs had bluer eyes than hose ;
England then measured men by blows,
    And measured time by candles.

The pilgrim bless'd his grateful shade
Ere Richard led the first crusade ;
    And maidens lov'd to dance
Where, boy and man, in summer-time,
Chaucer had ponder'd o'er his rhyme ;
    And Robin Hood, perchance,

Stole hither to Maid Marian ;
(Well, if they did not come, one can
    At any rate suppose it) ;
They met beneath the mistletoe—
We've done the same and ought to know
    The reason why they chose it !

And this was call'd the *Traitor's Branch*,
Stern Warwick hung six yeomen stanch
    Along its mighty fork ;
Uncivil wars for them ! The fair
Red rose and white still bloom, but where
    Are Lancaster and York ?

Right mournfully his leaves he shed,
To shroud the graves of England's dead,
    By English falchion slain ;
And cheerfully, for England's sake,
He sent his kin to sea with Drake,
    When Tudor humbled Spain.

While Blake was fighting with the Dutch
They gave his poor old arms a crutch ;

And thrice four men and maids ate
A meal within his rugged bark,
When Coventry bewitch'd the Park,
And Chatham ruled the Senate.

His few remaining boughs were green,
And dappled sunbeams danced between
Upon the dappled deer ;
When, clad in black, two mourners met
To read the Waterloo Gazette—
They mourned their darling here.

They join'd their boy. The Tree at last
Lies prone discoursing of the past
Some fancy dreams awaking ;
At rest, though headlong changes come,
Though nations arm to roll of drum,
And dynasties are quaking.

Romantic spot ! By honest pride
Of old tradition sanctified ;
My pensive vigil keeping ;
Thy beauty moves me like a spell,
And thoughts, and tender thoughts, upwell,
That fill my heart to weeping.

* * * *

The Squire affirms with gravest look
His oak goes up to Doomesday Book,
And some say even higher !
We rode last week to see the ruin,
We love the fair domain it grew in,
And well we love the Squire !

A nature loyally controll'd,
And fashion'd in that righteous mould
Of English gentleman ;
My child some day will read these rhymes,
She loved her 'godpapa' betimes—
The little Christian !

I love the past, its ripe pleasance,
And lusty thought, and dim romance,
Its heart-compelling ditties ;
But more, these ties, in mercy sent,
With faith and true affection blent,
And, wanting them, I were content
To murmur, *Nunc dimittis*.

F. Locker Lampson,
Hallingbury, April 1859.

A FEW OF OUR WORTHIES

'There is no treasure so much enriches the minde of man as Learning; there is no learning so proper for the direction of the life of man as History; no History that carries more weight of concernment with it than that of our own Country.'

'History hath this predominancy over Oratory and Poetry, that Oratory hath been rejected by the Lacedemonians; Poetry by Plato, Tertullian and others, as two pernicious instruments in a Commonwealth to pervert men's mindes; but History was never yet rejected by any; for what can be more profitable than to learn wisdom by other men's follies; to get experience by other men's cost and labours; and to be safe by other men's dangers. History is like a watch-tower, on which we may see dangers afar off, and so avoid them.'

'One calls History the Workmistress of Experience, and Mother of Prudence; it is the general Treasury of times past, present, and a lively pattern of things to come; it is that which reinforces Antiquity from her ruines, and makes the grey head of Time white again.'

'He that in conversation would be free,
Must be well read in various History.'

WILLIAM WINSTANLEY, *The New Help to Discourse*, 1669.

Saint Edmund

NEAR Ongar stands a famous shrine, the little wooden church of Greensted, reached by a straight mile of beautiful path and avenue. . . . The body of this church, once sequestered in the heart of the forest, is of roughly hewn logs, raised from the ground upon a brick foundation. The brick chancel is of later date, as also the wooden spire ; but it is believed that the timber nave was built in 1013, as a resting-place for the body of St. Edmund on its way back to Bury from London, whither it had been removed for a time ; so Greensted claims to be the oldest Church in Essex.

A. R. HOPE MONCRIEFF, *Essex.*

Saint Helen

WAS born at Colchester in this county, daughter to Coel King thereof, as all our British authors unanimously do report. She was mother of Constantine, the first Christian Emperour, and is famous to all ages for finding out Christ's Cross on Mount Calvary. Hence it is that, in memoriall hereof, the City of Colchester giveth for its Arms a Cross engrailed between four Crowns.

Saint Constantine

SON to the aforesaid St. Helen, was born also at Colchester ; one sufficiently known to all posterity by the mere mentioning of him.

Saint Ethelburgh

SISTER to Erkenwald, Bishop of London, was by him appointed first Abbess of the Nunnery of Barking in this county, by him built and endowed. Here she led a very austere life, and obtained the veneration of a Saint after her death, which happened 676.

Saint Osyth

SHE was the daughter to the King of the East Angles, and wife to Suthred, last King of East Saxons; by whose consent forsaking the world, she was veiled, and at last became Abbess of a monastery of her own founding at Chich in this county, until the Danes, infesting these sea-coasts, cut off her head in hatred of her religion. Yet this her head, after it was cut off, was carried by Saint Osyth (oh, wonder! oh, lie!) three furlongs, and then she fell down and died.

THOMAS FULLER, *Worthies of England.*

The Legend of St. Osyth

IS a specially interesting one, as showing the sanctity attached to the state of virginity in early Christian times. In the days of the Heptarchy, Osithe, or Osyth, was the daughter of Redwald, the first Christian King of the East Angles. . . . In early youth she vowed perpetual virginity, but was betrothed against her will to Sighere, King of the East Saxons. Before the marriage took place, or, as some have it, during the bridal feast, she stole away and took the veil. Afterwards she obtained from

Sighere, not only his consent to relinquish her, but the gift of the village of Chich in the Tendring Hundred (now St. Osyth) to maintain a nunnery. She was Abbess here until A.D. 653, when the Danes, under Ingwar and Ubba, sacked the convent and beheaded her. So much may be sober history; but now comes the miraculous element inseparable from the lives of the Saints. She picked up her head and, guided by angels, carried it to the church door, where she knocked and fell prostrate. At the spot where she was beheaded a fountain gushed out, long renowned for its marvellous curative virtues. The monks enclosed it in a monument and conducted the water through a leaden pipe, which remained until a modern yachtsman tore it up for ballast. Local tradition says that St. Osyth, head in hand, still visits the well and the church, a white ghostly figure, scaring travellers in the Nun's Wood.

REGINALD A. BECKETT, *Romantic Essex.*

de Luci the Loyal

ON the death of King Stephen (1154) de Luci, his well tried servant and companion in arms, attached himself to Henry II, having 'stood by the former in all the great crises of his stormy career, in the field as well as in the legislative chamber and on the judicial bench; at the same time his figure stands forth sharp and clear as the capable and energetic champion of all the liberties and rights of the Anglo-Saxon race against the tyranny of the Norman feudal aristocracy, for whose abolition he was to be one of, if not the chief, tool in the hands of the King.' . . . When the revolting nobles were beaten, Henry II placed his own garrisons in those castles of his lords which were not razed, and thus carried forward his long-sought purpose, the destruction of the feudal power, nor was even his most familiar friend spared, for de Luci had to resign Ongar Castle to the King. His intense devotion to Henry did not prevent him from opposing the King's enforcement of the cruel forest laws. In 1179 he resigned his high offices, to the king's great sorrow, and retired to a monastic establishment he had built at Lesnes in Kent, where on July 14th of that year passed away from this world, 'he of Luci, the wise, the prudent.' . . .

Let us think or dream what appearance his castle home presented in the middle of the twelfth century. Imagine, if you will, strong walls topping these earthen banks, and a circular keep of stone on the high mound connected with this lower court by a well-defended drawbridge. On the summit of that mound, within the keep, were the most important chambers, forming the last place of resort if the lower castle should be taken; this lower part occupied by the garrison buildings and stables, echoing to the tread of armed men. But the castle was not confined to this meagre space within these high walls; beyond in the meadows you may trace the course of ancient foundations, and away by the stream banks shew where outworks have existed, provided with their own water supply. Huge and imposing, no doubt, was de Luci's castle when Henry II was its guest in 1157. But I must ask you to travel back some 300 years or more before de Luci's time, and even then I think you would find these earthworks here—the great Norman and Plantagenet buildings were erected on earthworks that had had centuries in which to solidify. Here probably was a castle in the far away Anglo-Saxon days, when Dane and Saxon struggled for supremacy. Either may have thrown up this mighty mound and these earthen banks. . . . de Luci's Norman castle was not utterly destroyed till the days of Queen Elizabeth, when its ruins were pulled down and a house, perhaps the one now here, was built. From old writers' descriptions the Elizabethan mansion may have been on the mound, but I incline to think its main body was below, and that this farmhouse is part of it. Queen Elizabeth is credited with having visited more places than are entitled to claim that honour, but we know from Nichols' *Progresses* that she stayed here in July 1579, when the house belonged to William Morice. In 1744 Edward Alexander pulled down that part of the Elizabethan house which was on the mound, and erected a brick summer-house, domed and leaded, fragments of which remain.

I. Chalkley Gould,
Adapted from the *Essex Arch. Soc. Trans.*, 1898.

A Knight of Chivalry

SIR JOHN HAWKEWOOD, knight, son to Gilbert Hawkewood, Tanner, was born at Sible Heningham. This John was first bound an apprentice to a Taylor in the City of London, but soon turned his *needle* into a *sword*, and *thimble* into a *shield*, being pressed in the service of King Edward the Third for his French wars, who rewarded his valour with knighthood. Now that mean men, bred in manuall and mechanick trades may arrive at great skill in martiall performances, this Hawkewood, though an eminent, is not the onely, instance of our English nation. The heat of the French Wars being much remitted, he went into Italy, and served the City of Florence, which as yet was a Free State. Such Republiques preferred Forrainers rather than Natives for their Generalls, because when the service was ended it was but disbursing their pay, and then disbanding their power by cashiering their commission; such Forraigners having no advantage to continue their command, and render themselves absolute, because wanting an interest in Alliances and Relations. . . . Great the gratitude of the State of Florence to this their Generall Hawkewood, who, in testimony of his surpassing valour and singular faithfull service to their State, adorned him with the status of a man of armes and sumptuous monument, wherein his ashes remain honoured at the present day. Well it is that monument doth remain, seeing his Coenotaph, or honorary tombe, which sometime stood in the Parish Church of Sible-Heningham (arched over, and, in allusion to his name, berebussed with *Hawkes* flying in a *Wood*) is now quite flown away and abolished. . . . This valiant Knight dyed very aged, anno 1394.

FULLER, *Worthies*.

Death of the Great Earl of Essex

GEOFFREY DE MANDEVILLE, the most perfect and typical presentment of the feudal and anarchic spirit that stamps the reign of Stephen. . . . While marching to the siege of Burwell on a hot summer's day he halted at the edge of a wood, and lay down for rest in the shade. And lo! the very grass withered away beneath the touch of his unhallowed form. The fortified post which the king's men had now established at Burwell was a standing threat to the key of his line of communications. He was therefore compelled to attack it. And thus he was destined to die the death of Richard Cœur de Lion. As he reconnoitred the position to select his point of attack, or as, according to others, he was fighting at the head of his troops, he carelessly removed his headpiece and loosened his coat of mail. A humble bowman saw his chance ; an arrow whizzed from the fortress, and struck the unguarded head. . . . The tragic end of the great Earl must have filled the thoughts of men with a strange awe and horror. That one who had rivalled but a year ago the King himself in power should meet an inglorious death at the hands of a wretched churl, that he who had defied the thunders of the Church should fall as if by a bolt from heaven, were facts which in the highly wrought state of the minds of men at the time were indeed signs and wonders. But even more tragic than his death was the fate which awaited his corpse. Unshriven, he had passed away laden with curses of the Church. His soul was lost for ever, and his body no one might bury. As the Earl was drawing his last breath there came upon the scene some Knights Templar, who flung over him the garb of their order, so that he might at least die with the red cross upon his breast. Then, proud in the privileges of their order, they carried the remains to London, to their old Temple in Holborn. There the Earl's corpse was enclosed in a leaden coffin, and hung, say some, on a gnarled fruit tree, that it might not contaminate the earth, or was hurled, according to others, into a pit without the churchyard. So it remained for nearly twenty years, exposed to the gibes of the Londoners, the Earl's 'deadly foes.'

J. HORACE ROUND, *Geoffrey de Mandeville*, 1892.

Lucia de Vere

THE Countess Lucia, daughter of Henry de Essex and third wife of Aubrey de Vere, Earl of Oxford, founded at Hedingham, before the year 1190, a small Benedictine nunnery to the honour of the Holy Cross, St. Mary and St. James, and herself became the first Prioress. Weever, writing in 1631, gives an account of a document he had seen descriptive of the sorrow caused to the nunnery by her death. In it Agnes, who succeeded the Countess Lucia as second Prioress, asked of the Religious Houses of England their compassion and their prayers. It thus begins: 'May the soul of the Lady Lucy, the Head and Foundress of the Church of Holy Cross and St. Mary of Hedingham, and the souls of the faithful departed rest in peace, Amen'; and then goes on to record 'the showers of tears and flood of weeping' which the passing away of their beloved Mother, the venerated Lucy, first Prioress and Foundress of their House, had caused; her virtues and piety are mentioned, and then the new Prioress entreats 'the Monks and Nuns and Venerable Canons' to give their pity and offer prayers to the Most High, Who wipes away all tears from the eyes of His Saints, that He may have tender mercy upon the soul of His servant Lucy. To this application the religious of all houses answer in this form: 'May the soul of the Lady Lucy, Prioress of Hengeham, and the souls of all the faithful departed rest in peace. Amen. We have prayed for yours, pray for ours.'

'Upon the image of Lucy,' amongst other lines, were the following:—

Luci lucie prece lux mediante Marie
Luceat eterna, quia floruit ut rosa verna.

(Through the prayer of Mary may light eternal brighten the light of Lucia, for she flourished as the rose in spring).

SEVERNE ASHHURST MAJENDIE,
Family of de Vere, 1904.

Thomas Tusser

IT came to pass that born I was
Of lineage good, of gentle blood,
In Essex layer, in village fair,
That Rivenhall hight:
Which village lied by Banktree side ;
There spend did I my infancy,
There then my name, in honest fame,
Remain'd in sight.

* * * *

From Paul's I went, to Eton sent,
To learn straightways the Latin phrase,
Where fifty-three stripes given to me
At once I had ;
For fault but small, or none at all,
It came to pass thus beat I was,
See, Udall, see, the mercy of thee,
To me, poor lad.

From thence so sent, away I went,
With sickness worn, as one forlorn,
To house my head at Fairsted,
Where whiles I dwelt :
The tithing life, the tithing strike,
Through tithing ill of Jack and Gill,
The daily pays, the many ways,
Too long I felt.

When gains were gone, and years grew on,
And death did cry, from London fly,
In Cambridge then I found again
A resting plot
In college best, of all the rest,
With thanks to thee, O Trinity !
Through thee and thine, for me and mine
Some stay I got.

When all is done, learn this, my son,
Not friend nor skill, nor wit at will,

Nor ship nor clod, but only God,
    Doth all in all :
Man taketh paine, God giveth gaine,
Man doth his best, God doth the rest,
Man well intendes, God foizon sendes,
    Else want he shall.

Some seek for wealth, I seek my health ;
Some seek to please, I seek my ease ;
Some seek to save, I seek to have,
    To live upright,
More than to ride with pomp and pride
Or for to get in others' debt :
Such is my skill and shall be still,
    For any wight.

THOMAS TUSSER, *Five Hundred Points*, 1571.

John Ray

HAVING this Summer, Ann. 1691, with some diligence prosecuted the History of our English insects, and making collections of the several Species of each Tribe, but particularly and especially of the Butterflies, both nocturnal and diurnal, I find the number of such of these alone as breed in our neighbourhood (about Braintree and Noteley in Essex) to exceed the sum I last year assign'd to all England, having myself observ'd and describ'd about 200 kinds, great and small, many yet remaining, as I have good reason to believe, by me undiscover'd. This I have since the writing hereof found true in experience, having every year observ'd not a few new kinds. Nor do I think that, if I live twenty years longer, I should by my utmost Diligence and Industry in searching them out, come to an end of them.

JOHN RAY,
The Wisdom of God manifested in the Works of Creation, 1691.

JUNE 30th, 1702. It is true of late years I have diverted myself by searching out the various species of insects to be found hereabouts; but I have confined myself chiefly to two sorts, *viz.*: Papilios, diurnal and nocturnal, beetles, bees and spiders. Of the first of these I have found about 300 kinds, and there are still remaining many more undiscovered by me, and all within the compass of a few miles. How many, then, may we reasonably conjecture are to be found in England, in Europe, in the East and West Indies, in the whole world! The beetles are a tribe near as numerous as these, and the flies of all sorts not fewer. I have now given over my inquisition by reason of my disability to prosecute, and my approaching end, which I pray God fit me for. You that have more time before you may profitably bestow some of your spare hours upon such inquiries, and may probably make useful discoveries—at least may reap a great deal of pleasure and satisfaction in finding out and bringing to light some of the works of God not before taken notice of. So I heartily bid you farewell.

Mrs. Dale tells me that some friends at London talk of imposing a new task upon me, that is of describing such exotic insects as are found in the museums of the virtuosi about London; which, if there be no more able and better qualified person living in or near the City for such an undertaking, I should not be much averse from, if it please God to continue me any tolerable measure of health and ease, for that I may do sitting, and without much motion. As for our English insects, I think I may, without vanity, say, that I have taken more pains about some tribes of them than any Englishman before me.

JOHN RAY, *Letters.*

John Strype at Leyton

A few of Our Worthies

WITH a tumble-down vicarage, an impecunious parish and small stipend, Strype's task at Leyton, when he virtually became its vicar, was no easy one. He soon set to work, however, with vigour to get subscriptions not only for his own support but for the renovation of the church. The chancel was repaired in 1679, through the care, and partly at the expense of the minister. . . . When he obtained the Bishop's licence to perform the functions of a priest at Leyton, he was thirty-six years old. The long interval of fourteen years elapsed before any of his works saw the light, by which time he had attained his fiftieth year. Strype's works followed in rapid succession after his first publication, and one might well wonder how these ponderous tomes could be so quickly produced, were it not that the fourteen years of comparative leisure and freedom (at Leyton) combined with amazing industry, and zealous ardour for the work, furnishes sufficient explanation.

That Strype was attached to Leyton is strongly evidenced, not only by his care of the church, but more by his assiduity in collecting every scrap of information relative to its past history, as seen in his edition of Stow's *Survey*. He writes there as one personally interested in the history and antiquities of Leyton. . . . True antiquary as he was, he collected and focussed this history. It deserved focussing, for here, in this town on the borders of the river Lea (whence its name), formerly dwelt the proud and able Harold, the unfortunate hero of the battle of Senlac, on his four hides and a-half of land. Here also dwelt his rough and violent brother Tostig.

Essex in the Days of Old, 1898, Thomas Downs.

Archbishop Harsnett

MY village home of bright and younger days,
Chigwell! I fain would celebrate thy praise.
Though situate in county much despis'd,
Yet when men visit thee, they are surprised
That neither bog, nor waste, nor marsh, nor swamp,
Enfold thy grassy fields in fog or damp.
Thy bracing air, thy strong and fertile soil
Give health and food, as say 'the sons of toil';
And green old age, past three-score years and ten,
Vouchsafëd is to women and to men.

Thy antique Church, approach'd through groves of yew,
Upon the rising hill stands out to view;
Around its walls 'God's Acre' widely spread,
Contains beneath its turf the sleeping dead.

* * * *

And in its walls, on slabs of brass and stone,
Recorded are the names of some long gone,
Who, noted for their worth and deeds, have been
Throughout life's struggling lot and chequer'd scene!
Beneath thy paved and tesselated floor,
Sleeps Harsnett, Vicar, friend of rich and poor.

* * * *

His monumental brass on chancel floor
Records preferments that in all were four;
Of Chigwell Vicar—then by rapid rise
Two Bishoprics he fill'd, and soon a prize
Of England's Church he reach'd, 'Of York His Grace,'
Which last he gained when soon to end life's race.

His School for youths' instruction still is seen,
Its walls o'ermantl'd thick with ivy green,
Twice fifty boys and more make air resound,
As forth they go from task to playing-ground,
The classic works in dead and living speech,
Art, science too, the learned masters teach.

* * * *

That sons of poorer men should learn to read,
The good Archbishop Harsnett felt the need ;
A second school he founded by his will,
And all beneath the same roof learn'd, until
These days of change—for now, across the way
'The English School' apart from others play.
No longer free, each lad must pay his share
Of pence. This change would make poor Collier
stare.

* * * *

Long may God's Word of sacred truth be taught,
Nor time bring changes oft with evil fraught ;
Let Harsnett's will in this be e'er maintain'd,
That each poor boy in faith of Christ be train'd.

William Harvey

BUT incomplete fair Chigwell's fame would be,
Were name omitted, great as all agree,
Of Harvey—who descried in veins of man
That blood, his life, pulsating quickly ran.
In dining-hall at 'Rolls,' his portrait framed
Still holds a place with others greatly famed.
Of that same name was one more noted still,
Who list of Britain's heroes help'd to fill,
Brave Nelson's comrade in 'Trafalgar Bay,'
And shared with him the glory of the day !

'The Temeraire,' the ship in which he fought,
Gave signal proof that val'rous deeds were wrought.
At 'Rolls,' in entrance-hall, may still be seen
A trophy proud of what the day had been,
A fragment of his ship, with smoke all black,
Pierced by a ball, of which the hole shews track.

My praise of Chigwell now must have its close,
On thee may richest blessings long repose;
Ne'er may thy verdant fields be crowded thick
With streets and villas of unsightly brick!
But long remain a country village fair,
Where Londoners may roam to breathe fresh air!

W. S. H. MEADOWS, (1878).

John Morley of Halstead (1725)

TO wile away a couple of winter evenings spent in two of those picturesque hostelries, which a recent writer on Essex has described as a 'school of manners and a centre of culture,' this ex-butcher and land-jobber, friend of poets and protégé of noble and clerical patrons, determines to confide to paper the authentic history of his introduction to the financial world. Ignorant he remained, no doubt, of the self-revelation that accompanies his confession. Nothing could exceed his want of knowledge of commercial affairs outside his greasy butcher's block and blue apron to begin with; and yet, no sooner does he come under the spell of the great East India merchant than the clumsy Essex farmer blossoms out into the astute and wary speculator, adopting the language of the mart, and scenting afar a good investment or profitable bargain. How this change came about he relates with a singular naïveté, which shows him by no means undeserving of that title of humorist which Caulfield, in his *Remarkable Characters* has applied to him. Although near seventy years of age when he wrote his autobiography, Morley's memory never failed him. He reproduces conversations with his great patron; he recalls the details of his working clothes as well as of the finery afterwards bestowed on him, the quantity and length of his hair, the horses he rode, the lessons in deportment given him by Sir Josiah Child, and all the circumstances of his adventures thirty or forty years before.

He is ashamed of nothing and conceals nothing, not even his ingenuous panic at the ways of the 'morose-countenanced' London gentleman who designed, he was sure, to follow up his first small hoard of gold. The episodes of his career as a butcher are the very last things he is anxious to hide. He glories fiercely in his honest if unsavoury calling, and although not averse to sunning himself in the smiles of Countesses and Duchesses (as Pope in a letter humorously reminds him), he protests himself a butcher till his life's end. To show that his gory right hand had never lost its anatomical cunning, Morley kept up till he died the annual orgie of killing and scalding 'a hogg' in Halstead Market, paying for this privilege one groat as a fee.

CHARLOTTE FELL SMITH, *Merchant Morley*, 1903.

Thomas Day

'THE pool of mercenary and time-serving ethics was first blown over by the fresh country breeze of *Sandford and Merton*, a production that I shall ever be grateful for.' So wrote Leigh Hunt of the author of *Sandford and*

Merton, and it can well be imagined that there was much in common between the two. . . . Thomas Day, author of *Sandford and Merton*, *The Dying Negro*, and numerous political pamphlets long ago forgotten . . . was born in London on the 22nd of June, 1748. . . . Being after some time convinced that he had in his solitary Hampstead home sufficiently accustomed his 'eloquent' bride to those modes of life that he conceived to be essential to his happiness, Day, in 1779 proceeded to put into execution a long-debated project for the amelioration of the condition of the agricultural classes. . . . A house and small farm were found at Stapleford Abbots, about eighteen miles due east of London, in an intensely rural parish of Essex, that even now is sparsely populated, though the scenery is picturesque and the surroundings attractive, especially on the side of Havering-atte-Bower. . . . The house had only one good room, and the clay was of the heaviest description; it lies in the midst of old undrained forest land, and is to this day almost the worst part of Essex for farming; but to the enthusiastic Day such trifles as these were not worth consideration. The labourers' lot was to be easily improved . . . while the land was to be soon rendered fertile by a method of his own. . . . But, first the house had to be rendered fit for habitation, and true to his traditions, Day determined to carry out these improvements himself. . . . Numerous workmen were engaged and set to work, Day enthusiastically superintending their operations; but, alas! in a week's time he became tired of the newly-imposed task; it interrupted his daily walks with Mrs. Day, and prevented their long discussions in the neighbouring forest, or close application to books in the house. . . . Deep in a treatise written by some friendly agriculturist to prove that deep ploughing could render any land fertile, . . . the busy architect of his own farm was confronted by the master mason with the frivolous question as to where he would have the window of the new room on the first floor; Edgeworth was present and offered to assist, probably thinking that he might have to occupy the room, but the proffered help was disdainfully refused, and the mason was asked if the wall might not be built first, and the place for the window cut out afterwards. The workman . . . unwilling to disturb the harmony of the proceedings, willingly fell in with the new farmer's plans and built the room without any windows at all. Poor Mrs. Day had to use this room for two or three years as a dressing room, candles having naturally to be always lit in it, and it was then turned into a lumber room. The stay at Stapleford was short, the labourers proved ungrateful, the soil more ungrateful still, and Day left the clays of Essex for the lighter lands of Anningsley, near Chertsey, in Surrey. He got more land for his money here than in Essex, and was able to try upon a greater scale several of those doubtful experiments that he had found in foreign and other books, all of which, as might have been expected, ended in no inconsiderable loss of money.

MARK A. LOCKWOOD, *Nineteenth Century*, 1897.

Bramston of Skreens

THEREFORE, though I owne myselfe one of the most inconsiderable of subjects, and although I quitted my profession longe since . . . in the beginning of the warr which the two houses of Parliament made and raised against the Kinge, and lived without any imploye more then mannageing that estate conferred on me by my father, and some part acquired by my own industree, yet after the happie restauration of his Majestie Kinge Charles the Second, and for some tyme before, tho' I returned not to my profession, I was taken from my retirement, and putt into the service of my countrie, wherein I continued duringe three Parliaments in Kinge Charles the Second's tyme, as knight of the shire in two, and as burges for Maldon in the third, and which brought me into the 70th yeare of my age. When the last of those was dissolved, I thought it was high tyme for me to quitt all busines but that of dyinge and preparing for my death, and resolued with my selfe soe to doe; and, therefore, first I desired the Lords Commissioners of the Admiraltie to appoint another Vice-Admirall for Essex, which office I have held ever since the return of his Majestie. Soone after I alsoe made request to the Lord Chancellor, the Earl of Nottingham, that I might, with his Majestie's leaue, be discharged from the imployment of justice of peace; and to his Grace the Duke of Albemarle I made suite to be eased from the office of Deputie Lieutenant. And because I haue not hitherto binn able to preuaile in either, I shall be constrained, I feare, to giue dispensation to my selfe, much against my judgement, for I have alwaies thought the Kinge and countrie know best how to dispose of me, or any man, nor cann it befitt any man to refuse the commands and service of either. . . . Being now entred, when I write this, into the seauentie-second yeare of my age, I may very reasonably esteeme my selfe (tho' I feele noe disease nor the approach of anie) on the brinck of the grave, David, that King and Prophet, assuring us that threescore years and tenn are the age of a man.

SIR JOHN BRAMSTON, *Autobiography* (1682).

LORD DACRE . . . appears always to have been on the best terms with his brother-in-law, the Lord Chancellor Camden, and the rest of his wife's family. . . . The following story is told of himself and the Chancellor :—During a visit of the latter at Belhus they went together for a stroll, and in the course of their walk passed a pair of village stocks. The Lord Chancellor expressed a wish to see what it was like to be in them. He managed to get in but, when he had satisfied his curiosity, Lord Dacre found he was unable, without assistance, to extricate his brother-in-law, and so had to go for help, leaving the Lord Chancellor in this highly undignified position. Some time after, when a case arose before the court as to the nature of the punishment by stocks, Lord Camden said, with evident feeling, 'I have tried them, brother, and they are not pleasant.'

THOMAS BARRETT-LENNARD,
The Families of Lennard and Barrett, 1888.

The Taylors

A MORE complete literary family than that of which Isaac Taylor [third of the name] was the chief figure perhaps was never known. All of them were examples of heredity, whether as regards artistic taste or literary culture. Their lives were passed in the country; society for for them had no existence. The village life was enough. They sought no recreation that could not be found among green fields, waving woods, quiet streams, or hills far from the busy haunts of men. To do good to their neighbours, to improve their own minds, to secure an honest independence, was their only care.

J. EWING RITCHIE, *Essex Review*, 1898.

The Move to Ongar

WHILE it was still uncertain to what place her father might remove, Jane writes thus to a friend :—

'It is a strange sensation to survey the map of England without an idea as to what part of it we are to occupy. Yet, perhaps we feel less anxiety about it than you may suppose. Not to be further removed from London than we now are [Colchester], is our chief solicitude, and to be nearer would be very desirable; more especially on account of being able to see our dear brothers more frequently. For my own part, might I choose a situation, it should be a very retired one, among plain, good people whom we could love—a village, not a town. My love of quiet and retirement daily increases, and I wish to cultivate this taste; it suits me and does me good. To part with our house here—the high woods and the springs, will cost me a struggle; and more especially my dear, quiet attic. Might I hope to find such another in our next encampment, I should be less uneasy.'

The wishes Jane had indulged were, for the most part, gratified in the removal to Ongar, especially as regarded the house, its accommodations and its vicinity; and she once more enjoyed her room, which, though not an attic, was all she could desire. The Castle House, which my father occupied during the first three years of his residence at Ongar, was a most picturesque, old-fashioned abode, containing ample space for the pursuits of the family. It occupied a rising ground, just outside the ancient market town, and afforded that quiet seclusion which was so valued by its inmates. In the garden, perched on a lofty, well-timbered tumulus, and surrounded by a deep moat, stood some remains of the old castle, from which the house derived its name.

ISAAC TAYLOR, *The Family Pen*, 1867.

Tennyson in Essex

HIGH Beech, 1839.—I have been at this place in Epping Forest all the year, with nothing but that muddy pond in prospect, and those two little sharp-barking dogs.

Perhaps I am coming to the Lincolnshire coast, but I scarcely know. The journey is so expensive, and I am so poor. . . . The far future has been my world always. . . . I shall never see the Eternal City, nor that dome, the wonder of the world; I do not think I would live there if I could, and I have no money for touring.

High Beech, July 10th.—What a thunderstorm we had the other night! I wonder whether it was so bad at H—. It lasted the whole night, and part of the previous afternoon. Lewis Fytche, who was with us then, was looking out of my window about half-past 11 o'clock, and saw a large fire-ball come up the valley from Waltham, till it seemed to come quite over our pond; it then according to his account grew on a sudden amazingly large. 'How large?' I askt him: he said: 'like a great balloon, and burst with an explosion like fifty batteries of cannon.' I was so sorry not to have seen it, for it was a thing to remember; but I had just gone to my mother's room; she was grovelling on the floor in an extremity of fear when the clap came, upon which she cried out, 'Oh, I will leave this house; the storms are very bad here. . . .' Such a scene, almost ludicrous in its extreme.

All life is a school, a preparation, a purpose; nor can we pass current in a higher college if we do not undergo the tedium of education in this lower one. . . . Thro' darkness and storm, and weariness of mind and body is there built a passage for His created ones to the gates of light?

From Letters to Emily Sellwood, *Life*, 1897.

Dick Turpin

OUR favourite national freebooter was undoubtedly born at the Crown, then apparently known as the Bell, alehouse at Hempstead, in Essex. . . . Hempstead has not shown itself altogether insensible to the honour thus conferred upon it. It commemorates its illustrious citizen in the names of such landmarks as Turpin's Ring, Turpin's Corner, Turpin's Meadow, and Turpin's Oak near Dawkin's Farm, one of the numerous reputed hiding-places of the robber during his pursuit by bloodhounds. . . . The stories of all the highwaymen have been concentrated into a halo round this illustrious head. St. Turpin is the sweetest saint in all the Newgate Calendar. Every schoolboy in particular is a devout believer in Gentleman Dick, and the belief symbolises two very fine things: jumping five-barred gates, and the love of a gallant rider for a gallant steed.

Let the legend grow! It is one of the big verities of fiction, of Fiction which is so far greater and stronger than Truth! On clear nights, when the road winds upwards through dark copse and hollow to the dry and bracing upland, and spectral gates and railings reflect white light from the moon, my belief in Dick Turpin far outweighs my incredulity. I see the gallant outlaw dashing across the open, I hear the regular tlot-a-tlap of his horse's hoofs; I see the smoking breath of Black Bess, and watch the curve of her flanks as she stretches herself on the level turf. Forgotten are Thackeray and his cynical carpings, I am heart and soul with Harrison Ainsworth. I cheer onward his gallant robber and execrate the dastardly pack of his pursuers.

'Hurrah, o'er Hounslow Heath to roam,
Hurrah for the stilly hour!'

THOMAS SECCOMBE, *Essex Review*, 1902.

William Morris

IN 1840, when his eldest boy [William] was six years old, the family moved across the Forest to Woodford Hall, a large spacious mansion of Georgian date, standing in about fifty acres of park, on the high road from London to Epping. The park was only separated by a fence from the Forest itself; and the estate included about a hundred acres of farm land, sloping down to the little river Roding. Behind lay the pathless glades and thickets of hornbeam and beech which still, in spite of all encroachments, and of the nearer and nearer and nearer approach of London, remain in all essentials a part of primeval England, little changed in the course of hundreds, perhaps thousands of years. From the Hall the course of the Thames might be traced winding through the marshes, with white and ruddy-brown sails moving among the cornfields and pastures. The little brick Georgian church of Woodford (since enlarged and modernised), stood alongside of the Hall, which had a private doorway into the churchyard. On the roadside nearly opposite, on a green space now enclosed, were the pound and the stocks.

J. W. MACKAIL, *Life of Morris*, 1901.

Cunning Murrell

OF the relics of Cunning Murrell, the wise man of Essex, I have seen many, and I own some—his books of conjuration and geomancy, scores of his written horoscopes; and of his actual implements of magic I have seen the famous glass by which he, or anybody else, was enabled to see through a brick wall. This amazing instrument gained him vast consideration and authority among the unlearned of Essex up to and beyond the middle of the nineteenth century; but matter-of-fact examination, at a time when Cunning Murrell was altogether too dead to prevent it, robbed the wonder of all its mystery. For indeed, it was nothing but a simple arrangement of the mirrors in a wooden case, such as a schoolboy might make for himself with a little patience and the ruins of a shaving glass. But it served its turn well, and it was by this and other such aids that Murrell became, and remained to his life's end, something like absolute sovereign of all Essex outside the great houses.

But there was another instrument of far stranger purport. There was talk of it still, twenty years and more after its reputed possessor was gathered to his fathers and his twenty-one children in Hadleigh Churchyard. This was said to be nothing less than a strange disc of dull copper, by aid whereof Cunning Murrell could distinguish the true man from the liar. For the liar might stare at it till his eyes were sore, yet never could he see in it anything but its mere material self—a round plate of common dull copper; while it was the peculiar virtue of an honest man's eyes to perceive on the dim surface *something*—something of which only Cunning Murrell had the secret; something which the gazer must declare to him as proof and test of his truth. But of what that something was nobody could tell a word; for indeed it would seem that nobody had ever seen it. And yet belief in its existence was as wide as Essex.

ARTHUR MORRISON, *Green Ginger*, 1909.

An Essex Squire

BUT little remains to be told of John Archer Houblon [of Hallingbury, and Coopersale House]. Rich and prosperous, he had a keen power of enjoyment which gave zest to all he did, whether of business or pleasure, and if he never spared himself in the former, he did not stint himself in the latter. . . . A Tory of the Tories, and high and dry churchman of the old school, he was loyal always to the powers that be. He rebuilt the ancient white-washed church of Great Hallingbury, and spacious schools, . . . he would tolerate no tenant on his estates but that he was a churchman. But in spite of his intolerance of all encroachments upon his ideal, 'The Squire'—and all Essex gave him this distinctive title as he grew hoary with age and dignity—was humble and tender as a child in his efforts to break his faults and school his life to the standard of duty he held above himself; for he had, as his friend the poet wrote of him:

> 'A nature loyally controll'd
> And fashioned in the righteous mould
> Of English gentleman!'

He would bare his grey head to wind and rain if the name of God crossed his lips or those of his companion; and there are those who remember the zeal, if not beauty, of his singing in church. . . . And so, in a green old age, 1891, this chivalrous squire of a past that is gone, slept with his fathers.

LADY ALICE ARCHER HOUBLON,
The Houblon Family, 1907

Sir Evelyn Wood

I ATTENDED, on the 20th of September [1879], the sale of Sir Thomas Lennard's hunters at Belhus, then an annual event of much interest in the county, and it having been stated in the papers I should be there, many of the labouring classes came to see me. An elderly woman, who had walked many miles, pushing her way through the crowd round the show-ring, asked a policeman eagerly, 'Which is 'im?' She had pictured in her mind an imposing heroic figure in a splendid uniform, and on my being pointed out, a middle-sized man in plain clothes, observed in a disappointed tone, as she wiped her perspiring brow: 'What, 'im kill all them Zulus! Why, my old man would clout 'un.'

SIR EVELYN WOOD,
From Midshipman to Field Marshal, 1906.

OUR FIELDS, OUR DIALECT, SPORTS AND CUSTOMS

I smiled again, and said, 'Yea, but it shall not be so; not only shall men be multiplied a hundred and a thousandfold, but the distance of one place from another shall be as nothing; so that the wares which lie ready for market in Durham in the evening shall be in London on the morrow morning; and the men of Wales may eat corn of Essex, and the men of Essex wear wool of Wales; so that, so far as the flitting of goods to market goes, all the land shall be as one parish. Nay, what say I? Not as to this land only shall it be so, but even the Indies, and far countries of which thou knowest not, shall be, so to say, at every man's door, and wares which ye now account precious and dear-bought, shall then be common things, bought and sold for little price at every huckster's stall. Say then, John, shall not those days be merry, and plentiful of ease and contentment for all men?'

William Morris, *A Dream of John Ball*, 1888.

Shriek sea-gulls, while the gale doth billows roll,
And linnet warble to spring breezes kind;
Nature's true child thus opens wide my soul
To every wind.

C. Brizeux, *Anthology of French Poetry*.

Country Delights

Our Fields

NOW for the delight of our eyes, wee have the May - painting of Mr. Earth, with divers flowers of dainty colours and delicate sweets : we have the berryes, the cherries, the pease and the beanes, the plums and the codlings, in the month of June : in July the peares and the apples, the wheat, the rye, the barley and the oates, the beauty of the wide fields, and the labours with delight and mirth, and merry cheare at the comming home of the harvest cart. We have, againe, in our woods the birds singing: in the pastures the cowe lowing, the ewe bleating, and the foale neighing, which with profit and pleasure makes us better musique than an idle note and a worse ditty, though I highly doe commend musique, when it is in a right key. Againe, we have young rabbits that in a sunny morning sit washing of their faces, while as I have heard beyond the seas there are certaine old conies that in their beds sit painting of their faces : we have besides tumblers for our conies, and greyhounds for our courses, hounds for our chases, hawkes of all kinde for the field, and the river, and the wood: so that what can reason conceive that nature can desire ? but for the delight of both the country doth afford us. . . . And having all this, if we serve God withall, what in God's name can we desire to have more ?

NICHOLAS BRETON,

The Courtier and the Country-man, 1618.

Spring in a Meadow

Our Fields TO hear quaint nightingales, the lutes 'o the
wood,
And turtle-doves, by their mates woo'd,
And smelling violets sweet, how do these cheer
the blood!

* * * *

By rushy-fringëd banks with purling rill,
Meand'ring underneath the hill:
Thus, streamlike, glides our life to Death's broad
ocean still.

The pleasant grove triumphs with blooming May,
While melancholy sends away;
The painted quire on motley banks sweet notes
display.

Earth's flow'r—wov'n damask doth us gently woo,
On her embroider'd mantle to
Repose, where various gems, like constellations,
shew.

Ourselves here steal we from ourselves, by qualms
Of pleasure, rais'd from new-coin'd Psalms,
Where skies are blue, earth green, and meadows
flow with balms.

We there, on grassy tufted tapestries,
In guiltless shades, by full-hair'd trees,
Leaning unpillow'd heads, view Nature's ants and
bees.

* * * *

Then view the mower, who with big-swol'n veins,
Wieldeth the crookëd scythe, and strains
To barb the flow'ry tresses of the verdant plains.

* * * *

In neighb'ring meads, with ermine mantles proud,
Our eyes and ears discern a crowd
Of wide-horn'd oxen, trampling grass with lowing loud.

Next close feeds many a strutting udder'd cow ;
Hard by, tired cattle draw the plough,
Whose gallëd necks with toil and languishment do bow.

Near which, in restless stalks, wav'd grain promotes
The skipping grass-hopper's hoarse notes ;
While round the aëry choristers distend their throats.

EDWARD BENLOWES,
The Sweetness of Retirement, 1652.

Spring

THE Spring is dress'd in buds and blossoms sweet,
And grass-green socks she draws upon her feet.
Of freshest air a garment she cuts out,
With painted tulips fringëd round about,
And lines it all within with violets blue,
And yellow primrose of the palest hue :
Then wears an apron made of lilies white,
And lac'd about it is with rays of light.
Cuffs of narcissus her fair hands do tye,
Pinn'd close with stings of bees which buzzing flye
To gather honey-dew which thereto cleaves,
And leave their stings when they do prick the leaves.
Ribbons of pinks and gilliflowers makes ;
Roses both white and red, for knots she takes.

When she's thus dress'd, the birds in love do fall,
And chirping, then, do to each other call
 To sing and hop and merry make,
 And joy'd they all are for the Spring's sake.
But of all birds, the nightingal delights
To sing the spring to bed in warmer nights ;
Because the spring at night draws in her head
Into the earth, for that she makes her bed ;
And in the morning when asleep she lies,
The nightingal doth sing to make her rise ;
And calls the sun to open her fair eyes,
Who gallops fast, that he might her surprise,
But when the spring is past her virgin's prime,
And married is to old bald Father Time,
The nightingal, for grief, doth cease to sing,
And silent is till comes another Spring.

MARGARET (LUCAS) DUCHESS OF NEWCASTLE,
Nature's Pictures drawn by Fancies' Pencil, 1656.

A Country Life

THE country life is to be preferr'd, for there we see the works of God ; but in cities little else but the works of men ; and the one makes a better subject for our contemplation than the other. As puppets are to men, and babies are to children, so is man's workmanship to God's. We are the Picture, He the reality. . . . The country is both the philosopher's garden and his library, in which he reads and contemplates the power, wisdom and goodness of God. It is his food as well as study ; and gives him life, as well as learning. A sweet and natural retreat from noise and talk, and allows opportunity for reflection, and gives the best subjects for it. In short, 'tis an original, and the knowledge and improvement of it, man's oldest business and trade, and the best he can be of. *Our Fields*

WILLIAM PENN, *Some Fruits of Solitude.*

Clock-a-Clay—The Ladybird

IN the cowslip pips I lie,
Hidden from the buzzing fly,
While green grass beneath me lies,
Pearled with dew like fishes' eyes.
Here I lie, clock-a-clay,
Waiting for the time of day.

While the forest quakes surprise,
And the wild wind sobs and sighs,
My home rocks as like to fall,
On its pillar green and tall ;
When the pattering rain drives by
Clock-a-clay keeps warm and dry.

Day by day and night by night,
All the week I hide from sight,
In the cowslip pips I lie,
In the rain still warm and dry,
Day and night, and night and day,
Red, black-spotted, clock-a-clay.

My home shakes in wind and showers,
Pale green pillar topped with flowers,
Bending at the wild wind's breath,
Till I touch the grass beneath,
Here I live lone clock-a-clay,
Waiting for the time of day.

JOHN CLARE (1837).

Longing

Our Fields

OH, but to breathe the breath
Of the cowslip and primrose sweet,
With the sky above my head
And the grass beneath my feet;
For only one short hour
To feel as I used to feel,
Before I knew the woes of want
And the walk that costs a meal!

THOMAS HOOD, *The Song of the Shirt*, 1843.

The Country Side

MIDSUMMER in the country—here you may walk between the fields and hedges that are as it were one huge nosegay for you, redolent of bean-flowers and clover and sweet hay and elder-blossom. The cottage gardens are bright with flowers, the cottages themselves mostly models of architecture in their way. Above them towers here and there the architecture proper of days bygone, when every craftsman was an artist and brought definite intelligence to bear upon his work. Man in the past, nature in the present, seem to be bent on pleasing you and making all things delightful to your senses; even the burning, dusty road has a look of luxury as you lie on the strip of roadside green, and listen to the blackbirds singing, surely for your benefit, and, I was going to say, as if they were paid to do it, but I was wrong, for as it is they seem to be doing their best.

And all, or let us say most, things are brilliantly alive. The shadowy bleak in the river down yonder, which, ignorant of the fact that Barking

Reach is preparing for its waters—is sapphire blue under this ruffling wind and cloudless sky, and barred across here and there with the pearly white-flowered water-weeds, every yard of its banks a treasure of delicate design, meadowsweet and dewberry and comfrey and bed-straw from the bleak in the river, among the labyrinth of grasses, to the starlings busy in the new-shorn fields, or about the grey ridges of the hay, all is eager, and I think all is happy that is not anxious.

WILLIAM MORRIS, *Under an Elm-Tree*, 1891.

A Night in June

IN Summer — daylight fled — where flowers abound,
The fields their luscious fragrance pour afar,
With half-closed eyes, ears scarce awake to sound,
Slumbering, our minds not all unconscious are.

The stars, more pure, shine through the shadowy skies ;
Uncertain twilight tints th' eternal vault ;
Dawn, soft and pale, waiting its hour to rise,
Seems all night long on heaven's low ridge to halt.

HENRY CARRINGTON, *translated from*
VICTOR HUGO, *Anthology of French Poetry*, 1900.

Beans in Blossom

THE south-west wind ! how pleasant in the face
It breathes ! while sauntering in a musing pace,
I roam these new-ploughed fields ; or by the side
Of this old wood, where happy birds abide,

And the rich blackbird, through his golden bill,
Utters wild music when the rest are still.
Luscious the scent comes of the blossomed bean,
As o'er the path in rich disorder lean
Its stalks ; whence bees, in busy rows and toils,
Load home luxuriantly their yellow spoils.
The herd-cows toss the mole-hills in their play ;
And often stand the stranger's steps at bay,
'Mid clover blossoms red and tawny white,
Strong scented with the summer's warm delight.

JOHN CLARE (1837).

My Kingdom

HERE, with a fallen pollard for a throne,
Lord of the shelving pastures to the lane,
And ploughlands heavy with the hidden grain,
With noon just pulsing through the monotone
Of brooding skies, from cloud to clod alone
Save for the lark—my troubadour—I reign ;
Till slowly, from the distant hillocks wane
The elm-ringed homesteads and vague spires of stone.

Green England slips away into the dark :
The lessening slopes sink to the gorge of night,
And like grey monks the willows haunt the vale :
While abbey ruins glimmer through the park,
And lonelier than God-friended anchorite,
I tramp the furrows on the homeward trail.

L. CRANMER-BYNG, *An English Rose.*

Michaelmas Daisies

DAISIES on the emerald lawn,
Daisies rosy-white for dawn,
Rosy-white for summer's dawn,
Michaelmas daisies grey and drear,

Dusk for the dusky close of the year.
Michaelmas daisies for close of the year.
The year is old and the weary wind
Withers its glory, leaf by leaf,
Gone is the garland that April twined,
Gone, June roses, and August sheaf.
The apples are gone from the orchard boughs,
Faded the creeper's tangled grace,
The bitter blast from its rest must rouse,
For winter comes on apace, apace.
The old year dreams of its daisied dawn,
All golden bright and rosy white,
Dreams of its daisies like stars on the lawn,
And makes them again in the dusk of the night.

* * * *

Daisies on the emerald lawn,
Daisies rosy-white for dawn,
Rosy-white for summer's dawn,
Michaelmas daisies grey and drear,
Dusk for the dusky close of the year,
Michaelmas daisies for close of the year.

MARGARET VELEY, *A Marriage of Shadows*, 1888.

To our Impressionists

(*A School founded near Chelmer some ten years ago*).

'Pure colour is rest of heart.'—RICHARD JEFFERIES.

FOR charm discreet of river grey
Rimmed with small willows silver-green,
For velvet of a bankside way
Where many a childish foot has been,
For largess gold and Tyrian sheen
The wild sun scattered as he went,
I crave no outlines clear and clean,
I crave your hues of heart's content.

For sheaves of flutt'ring bronze so gay
For bright-dyed skirts of girls that glean,
For blue-eyed swains that dreaming stray
Where Chelmer runs the reeds between,
For stubble geese that plume and preen,
For mares with snow-starred foreheads bent
At shining ford in sundown scene—
Yours are the hues of heart's content.

For kindled clouds the light winds fray,
For dusky mill with poplar-screen,
For rose-beam of the sun at play
With bull's white flanks or brow serene,
For flash of river chill and keen,
For charms no draughtsman's lines present—
Dim plastic charms of Nature's mien—
Yours are the hues of heart's content.
School of our willowy stream, I ween
Ye walk the way more excellent—
Loathing stark shapes and contours lean,
Loving the hues of heart's content.

ARTHUR SHEARLEY CRIPPS.

A Rhythm of Spring

WHAT is it that makes me fling myself out into the Forest,
Alone but for the dogs that tear alongside or ahead of me?
What is it that makes me run shouting and singing down the slopes,
Jumping across the new brown mole-heaps in my way,
Feeling the keen east wind whistle round my ears,
Feeling the soft wet grass sink under my feet?
What is it but the Spring, the Spring, the Spring!

It is only February still, the trees are as bare as
December,
The dead brown fern rustles in the wind,
The dead brown leaves whirl and rustle around
the tree trunks,
There is nothing green but the small pushing
honeysuckle leaves,
And the vivid emerald green moss on the little
grass mounds ;
The turf is dun-coloured still where the snow has
crushed it.
Yet the sap is moving, is moving to meet the
Spring.

I hear the blackbird scold as he flies low along the
ground,
I hear the shrieks of the jay in the tree-tops,
I see the white tails of the rabbits among the
bracken,
And with a rush and a thud of little hoofs
Off down the glade the dark-clad deer go speeding.

Away in the heated church they are murmuring
Lenten litanies,
But something drives me out to be alone in the
Forest.
My blood is dancing with life, my feet cannot be
still.
Here is the great god Pan, here are the nymphs
of the woodland,
Dryads in every oak—another step will reveal them!
Here the old Earth-mother collects and revives
her forces.
Not much longer can they be held and controlled.
The sheer delight of life is in every twig and grass-
blade,
Even the slime-creatures send forth their orange
feelers,
Crawling over the trunks that have lain for many
a winter.

The Song of Spring is old, as old as creation,
Yet without fail it rises new and triumphant,
As the earth turns herself year by year to the sun-god,
And everything having life or breath wakes afresh and rejoices.

E. F. HOWARD, *Pagan Rhythms*, 1902.

These New-fangled Ways

(*A Ballad of Protest*).

ME, nao, sir, I don't howd 'ith these Board Schools.
Thäy larn the booys too much, my thinkin', now.
An' what I see, there's jest as many fools,
As when thäy put the young uns to the plough.

I ent owd-fashn'd, nao, I loike to see
The young uns comin' on. But nowadays
Thäy säy an' do sich things git over me,
An' I carn't howd 'ith these new-fangled wäys.

I howd 'ith larnin', mind, but let 'em larn
Saime way as I did, not that stuff o' theirs ;
Larn 'em the proper wäy to thetch a barn,
Larn 'em the wäy to sao a field o' tares.

Geoggerfy ! Now what on arth's the sense
A larnin' of 'em how the Moon go roun' ?
An' all about Ameriky an' Frence,
An' plaices tother side o' Lunnon town ?

My booy he come to me the tother night,
'D'yer knaow,' he säy, 'the Warld an' you an' me,
Are tarnin' on our axles—sich a raite
You woon believe? But there, tha's right,' says he.

I tarned he on his axles, you be boun',
  I cop he one. That maide me reg'lar riled,
That fairly did. The Warld a tarnin' roun'!
  To hear sich stuff an' nonsense from a child!

N'more I don't howd with them thingmibobs,
  Them Parish Councils wot they started now.
There's Tom an' Harry think they're reg'lar nobs
  'Cos they goo there, a-kickin' up a row.

Look at that Council meetin' here las' week—
  Why, bless my saoul! if Tom din taike the chair.
An' Parson settin' 'gin the door as meek
  As some owd sheep, I tell yer; that he were.

An' what d'yer think they done? Wh' nought, o' course,
  'Cos there ain't nothin' here want doin' to.
N' wonner Parson he look dreffull cross,
  Comin' away; I see him, didn't you?

An' I don't howd 'ith these 'ere ways at Charch—
  A-singin' o' the Scripters and that ere,
Dressin' theirselves in night-gownds stiff wi' starch,
  The Boible never tell 'em that, I swear.

They say *Ah*men instead o' *Ai*men now;
  Tha's on'y jes' to be contrairy like,
An' when that come the 'Glory be,' they bow
  An cartsey. Lor, I'd like to gim a shaike.

D' yer think the Aingels sing *Ah*men? Nit thäy,
  An' when these ere are dead an' gone, th'll see,
Th'll give it to 'em sträight up there; th'll säy,
  'You ent a-go'n to sing along o' we.'

I ent owd-fashioned, nao, I like to see
  The young uns comin' on. But now-a-däys
Thäy säy and do sich things git over me,
  An' I carnt howd 'ith these new-fangled wäys.

C. E. Benham, *Essex Ballads*, 1895.

The Old Essex Clerk

(*Selection*).

Our Dialect

HOW many Vicars have I seed? Best part o' half a score ;
But I be old and shaky now, and shan't see many more.
There's more changes 'mong the parsons than on the steeple bells,
And like enough there'll be yet more for anything I tells.

I've know'd parsons as walked to market and druv their own pigs,
And some on 'em rode a hossback, and some on 'em i' gigs.
Now it's pheaton or pony shay, wife, darters and all,
The bigger the young uns grus to, they make their father look small.

I've heerd Farmer Smith say, as he was threshing out a stack,
His missus 'ud use it all up and carry it on her back,
I've know'd rich Vicars and poor uns; I've seed both short and tall,
And our old burial sarplice is bound to fit 'em all.

It fares strange that ministers doant do their work by rule ;
I've often thought as parsons should go to a parson's school.
Some preached in the sarplice, I 'llows, because they hadn't no gownd ;
They warn't for scruples o' conscience, but took things as they found.

Our last Vicar — poor man — made a deal of preaching i' black ;
But there warnt no more in his head for that he had on his back.
He was one for the sarmint, and nit so much for the prayer ;
He wouldn't a clent the old place, but left it just as it ware.

Our church was holly choked up, and every pew was a box,
And every pew had jacks in it, as many as fleas in a fox.
For all the gals was peeping over the side at the boys,
Like bees in a bottle, the church kept buzzing with their noise.

The Churchwarden he heerd nothing, for he was sound asleep ;
He never minded the boys, least they was keeping his sheep.
First come my desk, then the parson's ; the pulpit top o' that,
Like yer neck, and then yer face, and then over all yer hat.

We sang then in the gallery, with fiddle and clarionet ;
If yer'd once heerd our band, sir, 'taint likely as you'd forget.
If the Parson should wish they'd change the tune by next Lord's day,
They pops flute and fiddle in bags, and goes right clean away.

William E. Heygate,

The Fugitive and other Poems, 1870.

'I Din Knaow'

(*A Ballad of Politics*)

Our Dialect

WARTY, he talk to 'em to-rights las' night—
I never h'ard a chap a-talkin' sao.
He säy the lan' an' all that is ourn by right,
But bless yer, *I* din knaow.

He säy we're all a poor, deown-trodden lot,
A set o' slaves—tha's fact, he towd us sao.
He säy we oughter hev I dunner wot,
But bless yer, *I* din knaow.

Good night! He give it to our Parson str'ight—
I reck'n if tha's right he'll hev to gao.
The Charch an' taithe are ourn, he säy, by right,
But bless yer, *I* din knaow.

I olluz sorter liked our Parson; thought
He wornt at all a bad un as the' gao,
Yet Mister Warty säy I didn't ought,
But bless yer, *I* din knaow.

Las' winter, when my poor owd missus died,
Parson he come to see us through the snaow.
Old Warty säy tha's on'y cos he's päid,
But bless yer, *I* din knaow.

He simd right kind to me and my booy Bob;
He sent us meat and things—a reg'lar shaow.
Goodstruth, our Parson! Who 'd a thought he'd rob?
Well, bless yer, *I* din knaow.

And Mister Warty, 'cordin' as it seems,
He bin our fri'nd these years and years agao,
A warkin' out for everlastin' schemes,
But dang it, *I* din knaow.

The las' elecsh'n, when them yallers found
  I wear'd a bit o' blew, they säy " Hulloa,
You ain't a go'n to wote for Mr. Round?"
  But I says, *I* din knaow.

Tha's what I olluz tell 'em when they praite,
  I carn abear these chaps wot cackle sao.
That fairly stop their jawin', don't 't, maite?
  Yes, tell 'em—You din knaow.

C. E. BENHAM, *Essex Ballads.*

Consulting the Oracle

I MET a mawther in the lane
    Larst Sunday night, and ever sin'
  I've felt a fever in mi' brain,
    And long'd to see that gal agin.

Somehow she knowed I liked her face,
    For she fared plazed as well as shy,
And my heart beat at sich a pace
    I let the chanst to speak goo by.

I count as she 'd jes come from chu'ch,
    But ef a meet 'ner she shed be,
I dunno that 'ud matter much,
    I 'd jine most any sex for she.

I 've bin a lookin' for a woife,
    Roun' these ere parts for years and years;
But she 's my mark—I 'd lay my loife
    She' fresh from somewhere in the sheres.

I wonder ef she 's got a buth,
    An' what ut is, an' whur t' be;
Ef I could get 'er, she 'd be wuth
    Her waight in suvrans most t' me.

It moighţ ha' bin her Sunday out,
But come nex' Sunday noight, I mean
Ter wear m' best, an' keep about
An' see her, ef she's t' be seen.

An' ef I see 'er, I shall say,
'Good evenin' dear, pray, how d' do?
We met, yer know, th' other day,
And I fell strayt in luv wi' you.'

This might fare sudden, but for me
The matter cou' n't come on too fast;
And 'ont folks cackle about we,
When they diskiver we bin ast?

But Sunday fared so long to wait,
And I s' wanted to be showed
What 's written in ther Book o' Fate
By somebody what raally knowed,

That I jes bin to Betsy Clark,
Fur she can read ut threw an' threw,
Says I, 'There's sixpence—keep it dark;
Now wass the best thing I kin do?'

An' Betsey Clark, she says, says she:
'Ax 'er, you 'll lose 'er ef yer dont,
That ool be, ef that be ter be,
An' ef that baint ter be, that 'ont.'

W. H. Harwood.

Molly Green o' Maldon

SWEET Molly Green o' Maldon town,
She lost her love so true,
When she was only seventeen
He left her for to rue.
He vowed with her again to roam
The green lanes blithe and free,
But she sits still on Maldon Hill,
While her true love 's at sea.

O, tell me, pretty fair nightingale ;
    Thou bonny brown bird sing,
And give me tidings of my love,
    The lad that serves the king ;
Your own true love, sweet Molly Green,
    Has sailed the Spanish Main,
And he stands on a poop of a fighting sloop ;
    Of that I am certain.

O, tell me, pretty fair nightingale ;
    Thou bonny bird so brown ;
What tidings of my other swains,
    All boys o' Maldon Town ;
Your other swains, sweet Molly Green,
    They each have got a bride ;
In storm and strife, the sailor's wife,
    Is the cutlass by his side.

L. CRANMER-BYNG.

THE traditions that were so common in my childhood among the old folk, their folklore and provincialisms, were full of interest. It would have been easy to reconstruct from them the history of the district and give, to a certain extent, the origin of the people. Many Anglo-Saxon expressions, for instance, are almost peculiar to Essex, and illustrate this. Such are rapidly disappearing, replaced by phrases more cosmopolitan, but far less forcible or exact. There is an expression frequently heard from old country folk which explains my meaning. It may be used in answer to a question: 'Have you seen John Smith lately?' The reply may be: 'Yes, I gave him the sœls of the day yesterday.' Now this word sœl is pure Saxon, meaning season or period. Therefore, in saying 'Good morning,' he gave the sœl, the time, the period of the day. Is not this far more expressive than saying he gave him the compliments of the day? The same word is used by Essex and East-Anglian persons to express the season for stripping off the bark of the oak, bark sœl; or the time of haymaking, hay sœl.

Another expression I have frequently heard will, no doubt, soon disappear. Ask an Essex or Suffolk woman whether the child she sends to the infant school can read or not. The answer will frequently come, 'No, she can't read, but she knows the chriss-cross row.' This means that the child knows and can read her alphabet, which was called the chriss-cross row because in the days of the horn-books the card enclosed in the horn case had the alphabet printed on it, with a cross in the first space as an invocation. Nothing in olden time commenced without this formula. Wills opened with an invocation; the physician began his prescription with one, the sign for Jupiter.

HENRY LAVER, *Essex Review*, 1902.

Song

'WAKEN lords and ladies gay,
On the mountain dawns the day,
All the jolly chace is here,
With hawk and horse, and hunting spear;
Hounds are in their couples yelling,
Hawks are whistling, horns are knelling,
Merrily, merrily, mingle they,
Waken lords and ladies gay.'

Waken lords and ladies gay,
The mist has left the mountain grey,
Springlets in the dawn are streaming,
Diamonds on the brake are gleaming;

And foresters have busy been,
To track the buck in thicket green ;
Now we come to chaunt our lay,
'Waken lords and ladies gay.'

Waken lords and ladies gay,
To the green wood haste away ;
We can show you where he lies,
Fleet of foot, and tall of size,
We can show the marks he made,
When 'gainst the oak his antlers frayed ;
You shall see him brought to bay,
'Waken lords and ladies gay.'

Louder, louder chaunt the lay,
Waken lords and ladies gay ;
Tell them youth and mirth and glee,
Run a course as well as we ;
Time, stern huntsman ! who can baulk,
Staunch as hound, and fleet as hawk ;
Think of this, and rise with day,
Gentle lords and ladies gay.

JOSEPH STRUTT, *Queenhoo Hall*, 1808.

The Epping Hunt

EXACTLY how the custom arose cannot be said. Our early kings were very jealous in guarding their hunting rights in the Forest. There is, however, a shadowy kind of story that one of our old kings, probably Henry I, granted the Lord Mayor and citizens of London the right of hunting in the forest. Certainly we know that the Lord Mayor did hunt there, but it might have been in a private wood belonging to him, rather than in the forest at large. Whatever may have been the actual right of the people to engage in the sport, the hunt annually took place on each Easter Monday down to comparatively recent times. The field of sportsmen assembled at Fairmead Glade; some on foot, some mounted on all manner of nags. A good forest buck was selected, its broad antlers dressed with ribbons, and as it was uncarted about midday it was seldom that a good run was not ensured, whatever might be the fortunes of the motley crowd that followed. The hunt is probably best remembered, because it formed the subject of one of Tom Hood's humorous poems. No doubt he wrote of what he had seen, for he lived for some time on the forest border at Lake House—which has recently been pulled down—on the edge of Wanstead Flats.

W. H. WESTON, *School History of Essex*, 1909.

Epping Hunt

NEXT once a year into Essex a hunting they go;
To see 'em pass along, O, 'tis a pretty show,
Through Cheapside and Fenchurch Street, and so to Aldgate Pump,
Each man with spurs in horse's sides, and his back-sword 'cross his rump.
My Lord Mayor takes a staff in hand to beat the bushes o'er,
I must confess it was hard work he ne'er had done before,
A creature bounceth from the bush, which made them all to laugh,
My lord he cried, 'A hare! a hare'! but it proved an Essex calf.

TOM D'URFEY, *Pills to Purge Melancholy*, 1719.

Fairlop Fair

IN the pleasantest part of Hainault Forest was the site of the famous East End saturnalia *Fairlop Fair*. The fair was held originally under the spreading branches of a great oak about a mile east of the Maypole Inn. Its reputed founder was a Mr. Daniel Day, an opulent block-maker of Wapping, who about 1725 commenced to give an entertainment, under the great oak, to his tenants and friends, at his midsummer rent collection. Day was a local celebrity, and the gathering seems to have grown into a fair before his death in 1767. After that, the mast and block-makers of Wapping regularly visited the fair, which was held 'on the first Friday in July,' riding there in two or three fully-rigged model ships, mounted on carriage-frames, each drawn by six horses, with postilions and outriders, and attended by music. The Fairlop Oak was famous long before Day's time. Gilpin, in his *Forest Scenery* (1791), writes: 'The tradition of the country traces it half-way up the Christian era. It is still a noble tree, though it has suffered greatly from the depredations of time. About a yard from the ground, where its rough fluted stem is 36 feet in circumference, it divides into eleven vast arms; yet not in the horizontal manner of an oak, but rather in that of a beech.' The once popular Fairlop Fair Song accounts in a very prosaic manner for the name:—

To Hainault Forest Queen Anne she did ride
And beheld the beautiful Oak by her side;
And after viewing it from the bottom to the top,
She said to her Court, 'It is a Fair-lop!'

Gilpin describes the Oak as overspreading an area of 300 feet in circumference. . . It was blown down in a gale in February 1820. JAMES THORNE,
Handbook to Environs of London, 1876.

A Morris Dancer

Sports and Customs

IN 1599 William Kemp attracted much attention by dancing the morris from London to Norwich; and as well to refute the lying ballads put forth concerning this exploit, as to testify his gratitude for the favours he had received during his 'gambols,' he published in the following year a curious pamphlet.

The third dayes journey, being Friday of the first-weeke. On Friday morning I set forward towardes Chelmsford, not hauing passed two hundred, being the least company that I had in the day-time between London and that place. Onward I went, thus easily followed, till I came to Widford-bridge, where a number of country people and many gentlemen and gentlewomen were gathered together to see me. Sir Thomas Mildmay, standing at his Parke pale, received gently a payre of garters of me; gloves, points, and garters being my ordinary merchandize, that I put out to venter for performance of my merry voyage. So much adoe I had to passe by the people at Chelmsford, that it was more than an houre ere I could recover my Inne gate, where I was faine to locke my selfe in my chamber, and pacifie them with words out of a window instead of deeds: to deale plainely, I was so weary that I could dance no more. The next morning I footed it three myle of my way toward Braintree: but returned backe againe to Chelmsford, where I lay that Satterday and the next Sunday. The good cheere and kind welcome I had at Chelmsford was much more than I was willing to entertaine; for my onely desire was to refraine drinke and be temperate in my dyet.

At Chelmsford, a mayde not passing foureteene yeares of age, dwelling with one Sudley, my kinde friend, made request to her master and dame that she might daunce the Morrice with me in a great large roome. They being intreated, I was soone wonne to fit her with bels; besides, she would haue the olde fashion, with napking on her armes; and to our jumps we fell. A whole houre she held out; but then, being ready to lye downe, I left her off; but thus much in her praise, I would haue challenged the strongest man in Chelmsford, and amongst many I thinke few would haue done so much.

WILLIAM KEMPE, *Nine Daies Wonder*, 1600.

Wild Fowlers

IN this inlet of the sea is Osey, or Osyth Island, commonly called Oosy Island, so well known by our London men of pleasure for the infinite number of wild duck, mallard, teal, and widgeon, of which there are such vast flights, that they tell us the island, namely the creek, seems covered with them at certain times of the year, and they go from London on purpose for the pleasure of shooting; and, indeed, often come home very well laden with game. But it must be remembered, too, that the gentlemen who are such lovers of the sport, and go so far for it, often return with an Essex ague on their backs, which they find a heavier load than the fowls they have shot.

DANIEL DEFOE,
Tour through the Eastern Counties.

A Poacher's Snare

ONE day I found a snare set in the hedge belonging to one of the farm labourers' gardens. I collared the snare. Then I took one of the cards that the huntsman sends me periodically, warning me to stop the earths. On the blank side of this card I wrote :—'And you must stop setting snares, Parker.' Then I signed my name at the bottom:—'John Wilkins, gamekeeper, Durrell's Wood, Standstead, Essex.' This card I stuck on to the pegs of the snare, so when Mr. Parker came to see what he had got he found a red card on the peg, and the snare was gone. This sort of thing cured the labourers of poaching just as well as a month in Chelmsford gaol, or a sovereign fine, and caused a much better feeling between us.

I came up to Mr. Parker when he was ploughing, and I said:—'I've lost a red card with my name on it, Parker; if you happen to run across it let me have it, will you?' So we would crack a joke over it, and I would quote the card :—'Please stop the earths for Wednesday.' Then I would speak to him seriously. 'You had better stop the hares from coming into your garden, Parker, by putting some bushes in the runs.' 'I will, keeper.' I never had any more trouble with him, and every now and again I used to give him a rabbit. 'Here's a rabbit for you, Parker, it will do a great deal better than an old hare, which would cost you a pound or a month in gaol.' 'A good deal better, keeper, and thank you kindly.' 'All right, Parker, my boy, but mind *that* doesn't happen again.' And it didn't.

JOHN WILKINS,
Autobiography of an English Gamekeeper, 1892.

With the Essex Hunt

ESSEX was the chief scene of my sport, and gradually I became known there almost as well as though I had been an Essex squire to the manner born. Few have investigated more closely than I have done the depth, and breadth, and water-holding capacities of an Essex ditch. It will, I think, be accorded to me by Essex men generally that I have ridden hard. The cause of my delight in the amusement I have never been able to analyse to my own satisfaction. In the first place, even now, I know very little about hunting—though I know very much of the accessories of the field. I am too blind to see hounds turning, and cannot therefore tell whether the fox has gone this way or that. Indeed, all the notice I take of hounds is not to ride over them. My eyes are so constituted that I can never see the nature of a fence. I either follow someone, or ride at it with the full conviction that I may be going into a horse-pond or a gravel-pit. I have jumped into both one and the other. I am very heavy, and have never ridden expensive horses. I am also now too old for such work, being so stiff that I cannot get on to my horse without the aid of a block or a bank. But I ride still after the same fashion, with a boy's energy, determined to get ahead, if it may possibly be done, hating the roads, despising young men who ride them, and with a feeling that life cannot, with all her riches, have given me anything better than when I have gone through a long run to the finish, keeping a place, not of glory, but of credit among my friends.

ANTHONY TROLLOPE, *Autobiography*, 1883.

Matching Green, 1883

SIR HENRY SELWIN IBBETSON,
An anxious face he wore,
As he watched the crowd that gathered
On Matching Green once more.

An anxious face he wore,
Upon the opening day,
For scores of horsemen had come forth,
From East and West and South and North,
All eager for the fray.

East and West and South and North
Have Dobson's cards gone out,
And Harlow, Chelmsford, Ongar,
Have noised the meet about.
Shame on the lazy sportsman,
Who lingers in his bed,
When the Essex hunstman and his hounds
To Matching Green have sped.

* * * *

Now grooms and second horsemen
Are pouring in amain,
From many a distant parish
Up many a muddy lane.
By many a famous covert
Where 'neath the farmers' care
At even shade the cubs have played
In the still summer air.

From the once royal forest,
Scene now of East-end larks,
From Romford, whence run early trains,
Heavy with City clerks.
From the long street of Dunmow,
Where, as the story's told,
The flitch was yearly given
To loving pairs of old,
From where the Stort meanders,
By mart of malt and flour,
From where conspicuous points to heaven,
The Epping water-tower.

* * * *

The duties of our office
  To-day let clerks fulfil,
To-day let others have our briefs,
  Or swell a client's bill ;
And in the haunts of Thespis
  To-night we'll not be seen,
Staring at pretty ballet-girls ;
  We're off for Matching Green.

* * * *

Now by the shade of Assheton Smith,
  It was a goodly sight,
To see some thirty horsemen
  Ride in the foremost flight ;
So flies a yacht, with topsail set,
  Running before a breeze,
So o'er our heads a driven bird
  Skims noiseless through the trees.

* * * *

And the last summons of the horn,
Sadly upon the breeze is borne,
The crowd that shone so gay at morn
  Melts gradually away.

But, Sportsman, as thou turnest
  Thy horse's head to home,
Think how thou mayest best maintain
  The chase in years to come ;
Remember to the farmer first
  We owe the fun all share,
Then ride over their acres
  With discretion and with care.

* * * *

And so for many a winter,
  The huntsman's horn shall blow,
And the merry music of the Hounds
  Sweep over the Essex plough ;

And ours be still a hunter
  That's fit to go the pace,
And ours on many an opening day
  To greet each well-known face.

And when some fellow sportsman's
  Hospitality we share,
And the inner man is sated
  With viands rich and rare ;
When, a glorious blaze of scarlet
  Round the festive board we sit,
And the oldest port is opened,
  And the largest weed is lit ;
And when over mahogany
  We all ride wondrous bold,
And of exploits in the hunting-field
  Some startling tales are told ;
And when affairs in general
  A rosy hue assume,
As wine and wit commingled
  Go circling round the room ;
We'll praise 'mid shouts of laughter,
  Loud mirth and racy jest,
While a glass of some choice vintage
  Stands brimming by each guest,
With three times three, and one cheer more
  To drink a bumper toast—
' Sir Henry, as the Master,
  Long may our country boast.
        Whoohoop ! '

ROLAND Y. BEVAN, *The Essex Foxhounds*, 1896.

The Dunmow Flitch

THERE can be few persons who have never heard of the Dunmow Flitch. It is enshrined for as long as English Literature shall endure, in Chaucer and Langland. . . . The gravest historians have given accounts of the beginnings of the Dunmow custom. There is Dugdale for instance, who was born in 1686. He writes in his *Monasticon* :—

'Robert Fitzwalter, who lived long beloved by King Henry, the son of King John (as also of all the realm), betook himself in his latter days to prayer and deeds of charity, and great and bountiful alms to the poor, kept great hospitality, and re-edified the decayed Priory of Dunmow, which Juga, a most devout and religious woman, had builded; in which Priory arose a custom, began and instituted either by him or some of his ancestors, which is verified by the common saying or proverb 'that he which repents him not of his marriage, either sleeping or waking, in a year and a day, may lawfully go to Dunmow and fetch a Gammon of Bacon.' It is certain that such a custom there was, and that the bacon was delivered with such solemnity and triumph as they of the Priory and Town could make—continuing till the dissolution of that house. The party or pilgrim took the oath before the Prior of the convent and the oath was administered with long process and much solemn singing and chanting.'

J. W. ROBERTSON-SCOTT,
The Strange Story of the Dunmow Flitch, 1910.

The Custom of Dunmow

A FOND couple make a vow before the Good Prior of the Convent of Our Lady of Dunmow, that they have loved each other well and truly for a Twelvemonth and a Day; and crave his Blessing.

'What seek ye here, my children dear?
Why kneel ye down thus lowly
Upon the stones, beneath the porch
Of this our Convent holy?'
The Prior old the pair bespoke
In faltering speech, and slowly.

Their modest garb would seem proclaim
The pair of low degree,
But though in cloth of frieze arrayed,
A stately youth was he;
While she who knelt down by his side
Was beautiful to see.

'A Twelvemonth and a Day have fled
Since first we were united;
And from that hour,' the young man said,
'No change our hopes have blighted.
Fond faith with fonder faith we've paid,
And love with love requited.

'True to each other have we been;
No dearer object seeing
Than each has in the other found;
In everything agreeing.
And every look, and word, and deed,
That breed dissension fleeing.

'All this we swear, and take in proof
Our Lady of Dunmow!
For she, who sits with saints above,
Well knows that it is so.
Attest our vow, thou reverend man,
And bless us, ere we go!'

The Prior old stretch'd forth his hands:
'Heaven prosper ye!' quoth he;
'O'er such as ye, right gladly we
Say Benedicite!'
On this, the kneeling pair uprose—
Uprose full joyfully.

The good Prior merrily bestoweth a Boon upon the loving couple; and getteth a noble Recompense.

Just then, pass'd by the Convent cook—
And moved the young man's glee;
On his broad back a mighty Flitch
Of Bacon brown bore he.
So heavy was the load, I wis,
It scarce mote carried be.

'Take ye that Flitch,' the Prior cried,
'Take it, fond pair, and go:
Fidelity like yours deserves
The boon I now bestow.
Go, feast your friends, and think upon
The Convent of Dunmow.'

'Good Prior,' then the youth replied,
'Thy gift to us is dear,
Not for its worth, but that it shows
Thou deem'st our love sincere.
And in return broad lands I give—
Broad lands thy Convent near;
Which shall to thee and thine produce
A Thousand Marks a year!

'But this Condition I annex,
Or else the Grant 's forsaken,
That whensoe'er a pair shall come,
And take the oath we 've taken,
They shall from thee and thine receive
A goodly Flitch of Bacon.

'And thus from out a simple chance
A usage good shall grow;
And our example of true love
Be held up evermo'.
While all who win the prize shall bless
The Custom of Dunmow.'

'Who art thou, son?' the Prior cried;
His tones with wonder falter—

'Thou shoulds't not jest with reverend men,
    Nor with their feelings palter.'
'I jest not, Prior, for know in me
    Sir Reginald Fitzwalter.'

'I now throw off my humble garb,
    As what I am, confest;
The wealthiest I of wealthy men
    Since with this treasure blest.'
And as he spoke, Fitzwalter clasp'd
    His lady to his breast.

'In peasant guise my love I won,
    Nor knew she whom she wedded;
In peasant cot our truth we tried
    And no disunion dreaded.
Twelve months' assurance proves our faith
    On firmest base is steaded.'

Joy reigned within those Convent walls
    When the glad news was known;
Joy reigned within Fitzwalter's halls
    When there his bride was shown.
No lady in the land such sweet
    Simplicity could own;
A natural grace had she, that all
    Art's graces far outshone:
Beauty and worth for want of birth
    Abundantly atone.

L'ENVOY

Hence the Custom

What need of more? That Loving Pair
    Lived long and truly so;
Nor ever disunited were,
    For one death laid them low!
And hence arose that Custom old—
    The Custom of Dunmow.

W. HARRISON AINSWORTH,
The Flitch of Bacon, 1854.

Lawless Court at Rochford

IT is kept at King's hill, in the yard of a house . . . Here the tenants kneel, and do their homage. The time is the Wednesday morning next after Michaelmas-day, upon the first cock-crowing ; without any kind of light but such as the heavens will afford. The Steward of the Court calleth all such as are bound to appear with as low a voice as possible, giving no notice when he goeth to execute his office ; he that gives not an answer is deeply amerced. They are all to whisper to each other. Nor have they any pen and ink, but supply that office with a coal ; and he that owes suit and service thereto, and appears not, forfeits to the Lord double his rent every hour he is absent. . . . The court is called lawless because held at an unlawful or lawless hour. . . . There is a tradition that this servile attendance was imposed at first upon certain tenants of divers manors hereabouts, for conspiring in this place at such an unseasonable hour to raise a commotion.

PHILIP MORANT, *History of Essex.*

King's Hill, Rochford

THE Court, though called Lawless, was actually recognised as a legal institution, and it is registered in the Court Rolls in curious old Latin rhyme. The following is an attempt to transpose the dog Latin into doggerel English.

By Royal Precept every year
The Lawless Court is holden here,
And by a custom which they 've got,
At this enlightened rustic spot.

That Lawless Court is summonëd
Before the sun is out of bed.
The Steward, with a piece of coal,
Ticks off the tenants' rental roll,
As soon as he may chance to hear
Some extra wakeful chanticleer;
Which sound shall he the only sort
Of summons to the Lawless Court.
For then the aforesaid steward's got to
Call, in a *voce*, very *sotto*,
Each tenant who must make reply
Or else he pays the penalty:
Moreover he must pay, I ween
Unless he can approach unseen.
The man who dares a light to bring
Breaks through the rules like anything;
And he who does not bring a light
Is also in a sorry plight.
Without regard to equity
The Court adjudicates each plea.

The Essex Notebook, 1884.

The Knighting of the Loin of Beef

THAT interesting ceremony known as the Knighting of the Loin of Beef belongs to the Essex Forest. According to an old rhyme—

'The Second Charles of England
Rode forth one Christmastide
To hunt a gallant stag often,
Of Chingford Woods the pride.'

The hunt was cut short by a snowstorm which sent the party for shelter to Friday Hall, a mansion overlooking the Lea Valley from Friday Hill, near Chingford Hatch, about nine miles from the city. Blazing logs and good cheer, conducted on a scale of prodigal hospitality, restored the good humour of the Monarch. From a huge loin of beef he filled his plate—some say using his sword for a knife—

'Quoth Charles: Odds fish! a noble dish,
And noble made by me,
By kingly right, I dub thee knight—
Sir Loin—henceforward be.'

P. J. S. PERCEVAL, *London's Forest.*

The Yearly Distress, or Tithing-Time at Stock

'Verses addressed to a country clergyman, complaining of the disagreeableness of the day annually appointed for receiving the dues at the Parsonage.'

COME, ponder well, for 'tis no jest,
To laugh it would be wrong,
The troubles of a worthy priest,
The burden of my song.

This priest he merry is and blithe
Three quarters of a year,
But oh! it cuts him like a scythe,
When tithing-time draws near.

He then is full of fright and fears,
As one at point to die,
And long before the day appears
He heaves up many a sigh.

For then the farmers come jog, jog
  Along the miry road,
Each heart is heavy as a log,
  To make their payments good.

In sooth, the sorrow of such days
  Is not to be express'd,
When he that takes and he that pays
  Are both alike distress'd.

Now all unwelcome at his gates
  The clumsy swains alight,
With rueful faces and bald pates—
  He trembles at the sight.

* * * *

So in they come—each makes his leg,
  And flings his head before,
And looks as if he came to beg
  And not to quit a score.

* * * *

The dinner comes, and down they sit:
  Were e'er such hungry folk?
There's little talking, and no wit,
  It is no time to joke.

One wipes his nose upon his sleeve,
  One spits upon the floor,
Yet, not to give offence or grieve,
  Holds up the cloth before.

. . . . .

At length the busy time begins,
  Come neighbours, we must wag—
The money chinks, down drop their chins,
  Each lugging out his bag.

One talks of mildew and of frost,
  And one of storm and hail,
And one of pigs, that he has lost
  By maggots at the tail.

Quoth one, 'A rarer man than you
  In pulpit none shall hear :
But yet, methinks, to tell you true,
  You sell it plaguey dear.'

O why are farmers made so coarse,
  Or clergy made so fine?
A kick, that scarce would move a horse,
  May kill a sound divine.

Then let the boobies stay at home ;
  'Twould cost him, I dare say,
Less trouble taking twice the sum,
  Without the clowns that pay.

WILLIAM COWPER, (1780).

Election Humours

IN old times men were merry, and made fun even of an election ; at any rate they did this in Chelmsford, where at every county election a mock contest was held on a small island between the two rivers known as Mesopotamia ('that blessed word,' as the old woman said when she heard it in the course of her favourite parson's sermon). At this mock election, we are told, after the successful candidate was chaired with every mark of honour, he was ducked in the stream. Sometimes one wishes that old customs were revived. I know, at any rate, more than one candidate who, if he were ducked in the stream and left there, would be little missed by an enlightened public, such as we have in the present age.

J. EWING RITCHIE,
Some of Our East Coast Towns, 1893.

Bee Lore

Old Customs

I REMEMBER when I was a school-boy in Essex, my father being then curate of a country parish not far from Colchester, the news came that the rector was dead, which, of course, implied the consequent removal, after a space of weeks or months, of the curate. But that did not affect me, or fix itself upon my attention as did the proceedings taken in connection with the bees, of which a large stock belonged to the rectory. I cannot remember who the person acting on behalf of the rectorial family was, or by what authority the said person acted; but I do remember the key of the main door of the house being taken—together with sundry strips of some black material, and a kind of procession organised for a formal visit to the bee-stand. And when it was reached, the bearer of the key proceeded to bind a black strip round each hive. This was called 'putting the bees into mourning,' and as each strip was knotted, three taps with the key were given, and each hive severally informed that the master was dead. There was a sort of weird solemnity about the whole proceeding which produced a lasting impression on my mind.

JOHN CHRISTOPHER ATKINSON,

Forty Years in a Moorland Parish, 1891.

OUR POETS ON LOVE, FRIENDSHIP AND THE VIRTUES

Let the foundation of thy affection be vertue, then make the building as rich and glorious as thou canst: if the foundation be beauty or wealth and the building vertue, the foundation is too weak for the building; and it will fall. Happy is he, the pallace of whose affection is founded upon vertue, wall'd with riches, glaz'd with beautie, and roof'd with honor.

F. QUARLES, *Enchiridion.*

There can be no friendship where there is no freedom. Friendship loves a free air, and will not be penned up in straight and narrow enclosures. It will speak freely, and act so too; and take nothing ill where no ill is meant; nay, where it is, 'twill easily forgive, and forget too, upon small acknowledgments.

WILLIAM PENN, *Fruits of Solitude.*

Rings and true friends are without ends.

WILLIAM WINSTANLEY, *New Help to Discourse.*

O, that I were a christall glasse,
For her to behoulde her angells face
Continually in :
O, that I were sum princely vesture,
Her most noble bodye allwayes to cover,
And ever to be neare her skin.
Withowte any mocke,
Woold God I were her smock ;
Else woulde I were a bathe,
Or sweete compounde water,
Her delicate limmes to baathe,
Both sooner and later.
On condition her grace would dayne
To weare me and not to teare me :
God forbidd, I should disdeyne
To become her pantocle.
I would wish to be her very shooe,
Wheresoever she chance to gooe.
Or any other thinge,
And specially her best ringe,
To be alwayes in her præsence,
Where herselfe hath residence.

GABRIEL HARVEY, *The Scholar's Love*, (1575).

FOOLISH love is onely folly,
Wanton love is too unholly :
Greedy love is covetous,
Idle love is frivolous,
But the gratious love is it :
That doth proove the worth of wit.

Beautie but deceives the eye,
Flatterie leades the eare awrye :
Wealth doth but inchaunt the wit,
Want the overthrow of it.
While in wisdomes worthy grace,
Vertue sees the sweetest face.

On Love

There hath love found out his life,
Peace without all thought of strife :
Kindenes in discretions care,
Truth that clearly doth declare.
Faith doth in true fancy proove,
Lust the excrement of love.

Then in faith my fancie see
How my love may construed bee,
How it growes and what it seekes,
How it lives and what it likes.
So in highest grace regarde it
Or in lowest scorn discarde it.

NICHOLAS BRETON,
The Passionate Shepherd, 1604.

Song

DEAREST, if I by my diserning,
May maintain in your thoughts my love,
Let me it still enjoy ;
Nor faith destroy :
But pitty Love where it doth move.

Let no other new Love invite you
To leave me who so long have serv'd :
Nor let your power decline,
But purely shine
On me who have all truth preserv'd.

Or had you once found my heart straying,
Then would not I accuse your change,
But being constant still,
It needs must kill
One, whose soule knowes not how to range.

Yet may you Love's sweet smiles recover,
Since all love is not yet quite lost,
But tempt not Love too long,
Lest so great wrong
Make him thinke he is too much crost.

LADY MARY WROTH, *Urania*, 1621.

LOVE is a noble passion of the heart, *On Love*
That with its very essence doth impart
All needfull circumstances and effects
Unto the chosen party it affects ;
In absence, it enjoys ; and with an eye,
Fill'd with celestial fire, doth espy
Objects remote : it joys and smiles in grief ;
It sweetens poverty ; it brings relief ;
It gives the feeble, strength ; the coward, spirit ;
The sick man, health ; the undeserving, merit ;
It makes the proud man humble ; and the stout
It overcomes, and treads him under foot ;
It makes the mighty man of war to droop ;
And him to serve, that never yet could stoop ;
It is a fire whose bellows are the breath
Of Heaven above, and kindled here beneath :
'Tis not the power of a man's election
To love ; he loves not by his own direction ;
It is nor beauty, nor benign aspect,
That always moves the lover to affect ;
These are but means : Heaven's pleasure is the
cause :
Love is not bound to reason, and her laws
Are not subjected to the imperious will
Of man : it lies not in his power to will.

F. QUARLES, *The History of Samson*, 1631.

How to Treat a Wife

IF thy fancy and judgment have agreed in the choice of a fit wife, be not too fond, lest she surfeit, nor too peevish, lest she languish. Love so, that thou mayst be fear'd : rule so, that thou mayst be honour'd. Be not too diffident, lest thou teach her to deceive thee, nor too suspicious, lest thou teach her to abuse thee. If thou see a fault, let thy love hide it ; if she continue it, let thy wisdom reprove it: reprove her not openly, lest she grow bold. Rebuke her not tauntingly, lest she grow spiteful. Proclaim not her beauty, lest she grow proud; boast not her wisdom, lest thou be thought foolish. Shew her not thy imperfections lest she distain thee. Pry not into her dairy, lest she despise thee. Prophane not her ears with loose communication, lest thou defile the sanctuary of her modesty. An understanding husband makes a discreet wife, and she, a happy husband.

F. QUARLES, *Enchiridion.*

A Song by a Lady

YE virgin powers defend my heart
From am'rous looks and smiles,
From sawcy love, or nicer art,
Which most our sex beguiles.

From sighs and vows, from awful fears,
That do to pity move,
From speaking silence, and from tears,
Those springs that water love.

But if through passion I grow blind
Let honor be my guide;
And where frail nature seems inclin'd
There place a guard of pride.

An heart whose flames are seen, tho' pure,
Needs every virtue's aid;
And she who thinks herself *secure*,
The soonest is betray'd.

From *The Virgin Muse*, 1717.

From Buondelmonte

On Love

LOVE smiles and lurks unheeded oft
In friendship's form, his end to gain;
Then mingling and confounding soft
With stern, he's rancour and disdain;
To pity, too, himself he changes;
Of sport and spite assumes the name:
But in whatever shape he ranges
Love is he always, just the same.

C. LESINGHAM SMITH, *Odes and Sonnets*, 1842.

January

FROM this dull rainy undersky and low,
This murky ending of a leaden day,
That never knew the sun, this half-thawed snow,
These tossing black boughs faint against the grey
Of gathering night, thou turnest, dear, away
Silent, but with thy scarce-seen kindly smile
Sent through the dusk my longing to beguile.

There, the lights gleam, and all is dark without!
And in the sudden change our eyes meet dazed—
O look, love, look again! the vail of doubt
Just for one flash, past counting, then was raised!
O eyes of heaven, as clear thy sweet soul blazed
On mine a moment! O come back again
Strange rest and clear amid the long dull pain!

Nay, nay, gone by, though there she sitteth still,
With wide grey eyes so frank and fathomless—
Be patient, heart, thy days they yet shall fill
With utter rest. Yea, now thy pain they bless,

And feel thy last hope of the world's redress—
O unseen hurrying rack ! O wailing wind !
What rest and where go ye this night to find ?

WILLIAM MORRIS, *The Earthly Paradise*, 1870.

Triolets

I wish I could recall the day
When you and I were first together !
My heart insists the month was May ;
I wish I could recall the day,
The very hour and minute—nay,
The passing mood of wind and weather.
I wish I could recall the day
When you and I were first together !

It's best to smile and hide our tears,
For so the old world wags more gaily ;
All men alike have secret fears,
It's best to smile and hide our tears,
For where a jocund face appears
There other hearts take courage daily,
It's best to smile and hide our tears,
For so the old world wags more gaily.

E. F. HOWARD, *Verses*, 1901.

A Name

I must not name thy name, Yet all day long
It holds a place within my secret heart,
In crowded rooms or when I walk apart
It haunts me like the echo of a song,
A presence more familiar and more strong

Than all the daily faces that I meet ;
My inmost stronghold and my calm retreat
When weary and dismayed by doubt or wrong.
Never I turn my face where duty tends,
Or pause to view the work my hands have wrought,
But silently I weigh thy praise or blame.
Never a morning breaks or night descends,
But, when I kneel to pray, swifter than thought
Or will of mine, there springs to heaven thy name.

E. F. HOWARD.

Eternal Love

LOVE to the master, and the mate
Stirs itself feebly in Life's lowest sphere ;
That to our parent, and the bed
More large extends, and breathes a life of sense ;
That to our country, and its sire
Self raises loftier in Reason's air :
But, that to God,
Ravished with ecstasy, itself transcends,
Nor bounds, nor limits would it own ;
But, narrow'd that (like lovers kept apart)
Warms, heats, yea boils, boils up and over !
Longs for th' Eternal, sighs for Him, beyond that lover !

EDWARD BENLOWES, *Theophila*, 1652.

The Perfect Friend

BEWARE of had I wist, whose fine brings care and smart,
Esteeme of all as they deserve, and deeme as deemde thou art ;
So shall thy perfect frend enjoy his hoped hire,
And faithless faunyng foe shall misse th'effect of his desire ;

Goodwill shall have his gayne, and hate shall
heape despight ;
A faithlesse frend shall finde distrust, and love
shall reape delight.
Thyselfe shall rest in peace, thy frend shall joy
thy fate,
Thy foe shall fret at thy good happe, and I shall
joy thy state ;
But this my fond advise may seeme perchaunce
but vayne,
As rather teaching how to lose than how a frend
to gayne.
But 'tis not my intent to teach to finde a frende,
But safely how to love and live, is all that I
intende ;
And if you prove in part, and find my cousell
true,
Then wish me well for my good will, 'tis all I
crave ; adieu,
My lucke is losse.

GEORGE GASCOIGNE, 1578.

THE perfect model of true Friendship's this :
A rare affection of the soul, which is
Begun with ripened judgment ; doth
persever
With simple wisdom, and concludes with never.
Tis pure in substance, as refinëd gold,
That buyeth all things, but is never sold.
It is a coin, and most men walk without it ;
True Love's the stamp Jehovah's writ about it ;
It rusts unus'd, but using makes it brighter,
'Gainst Heaven high treason 'tis, to make it
lighter.
'Tis a gold chain, links soul and soul together
In perfect unity, ties God to either.

Affliction is the touch, whereby we prove,
Whether't be gold, or gilt with feignëd Love.
The wisest moralist that ever div'd
Into the depths of Nature's bowels, striv'd
With th' augur of experience to bore
Men's hearts so far, till he had found the ore
Of Friendship, but, despairing of his end,
My friends (said he) there is no perfect friend.
Friendship's like Musick; two strings tun'd alike,
Will both stir; though only one you strike.
It is the quintessence of all perfection
Extracted into one; a sweet connexion
Of all the virtues, moral and divine,
Abstracted into one. It is a Mine
Whose nature is not rich, unless in making
The state of others wealthy by partaking:
It blooms and blossoms, both in sun and shade,
Doth (like the bay in winter) never fade:
It loveth all, and yet suspecteth none,
Is provident, yet seeking not her own:
'Tis rare itself, yet maketh all things common,
And is judicious, yet judgeth no man.

* * * *

It is no wise man's part to weigh a Friend,
Without the gloss and goodness of his end:
For life, without the death considered, can
Afford but half a story of the man.
'Tis not my friend's affliction that shall make
Me either wonder, censure, or forsake:
Judgment belongs to Fools; enough that I
Find he's afflicted, not enquire, why:
It is the hand of Heaven; that self-same sorrow,
Grieves him to-day, may make me groan to-[morrow.
Heaven be my comfort; in my highest grief,
I will not trust to man's, but Thy, relief.

QUARLES, *Divine Poems.*

On Friendship

On Friendship

DELIBERATE long before thou consecrate a friend; and when thy impartiall judgement concludes him worthy, receive him joyfully, and entertain him wisely; impart thy secrets boldly, and mingle thy thoughts with his. He is thy very self, and use him so; if thou firmly think him faithfull, thou mak'st him so.

With three sorts of men enter no serious friendship: the ungratefull man; the multiloquious man; the coward. The first cannot prize thy favours; the second cannot keep thy counsel; the third dare not vindicate thy honour.

Convey thy love to thy friend as an arrow to the mark, to stick there; not as a ball against the wall, to rebound back to thee: that friendship will not continue to the end that is begun for an end.

He that professes himself thy open enemy, arms thee against the evill he means thee, but he that dissembles himself thy secret friend, strikes beyond caution, and wounds above cure. From the first, thou mayst deliver thyself; from the last, good Lord deliver thee.

QUARLES, *Enchiridion*.

The Service of Friendship

IT is, however, the mutual exchange of friendship that forms one of the most pleasing features of civilized society, and of practical christianity. I must think that christianity is unknown, as to its proper influence when there is no disposition to oblige a friend, or even when there is not a willingness to submit to some difficulty and inconvenience for the sake of doing it. . . . The liberal man deviseth liberal things, and great is his reward; when any request is made to him, he listens with cheerfulness ; if he accidentally hear of any circumstance, in the situation of a friend or a neighbour, that requires attention, he will offer his aid, even unasked; he will bear some inconvenience himself, and even enjoy a personal disappointment, when by submitting to it he can effectually serve a fellow creature.

STEPHEN MORELL,
The Excursions of Vigilius, 1813.

To a Distant Friend

WE do not want for friendships, you and I,
And through the accidents of time and place
It seldom chances we are face to face
As the strong tide of busy life rolls by.
But though we own full many a nearer tie,
Though other lives with ours more closely twine
Than ever mine with yours or yours with mine,
Yet never doubt or let the world deny
That there is something where our paths have crossed
Which cannot be confused with aught beside,
Distinct and fragrant, permanent and true ;
What we have gained and given is not lost.
Nothing can spoil or change, whate'er betide.
Just what you are to me, and I to you.

E. F. HOWARD.

Fair Dealing

IF any flower that here is grown,
Or any herb, may ease your pain,
Take and account it as your own,
But recompense the like again ;
For some and some is honest play,
And so my wife taught me to say.

If here to walk you take delight,
  Why, come, and welcome when you will:
If I bid you sup here this night,
  Bid me another time, and still
Think some and some is honest play,
For so my wife taught me to say.

Thus, if you sup or dine with me,
  If you walk here, or sit at ease;
If you desire the thing you see,
  And have the same your mind to please,
Think some and some is honest play,
And so my wife taught me to say.

GEORGE GASCOIGNE, *Gardenings* (1575).
Written at the end of his 'Close Walk.'

Joy and Tears

A SIGHE sometymes maye ease a swellinge harte,
  As soden blastes do cleare the clowdye skyes
And teares lickwyse maye somewhatt ease some smarte,
  As showers allaye the dusts from earthe wch ryse,
For thinges (which byde extremytye) be glade,
To feele the leaste relyef that may be hade.

Butt as the rayne which dothe ensew such blaste
  From heaven on high wth greater force dothe fall,
And as the duste, when little droppes be paste
  Dothe quickly drye, and much encrease wth all,
So sighes and teares (yf soveraigne grace be greeved)
Consume the harte, whose lightes they earst relieved.

GEORGE GASCOIGNE, *Epilogismus* (1575).

WELL may we cry with that old Grecian bard, *On the Virtues*
Whoe'er he was—who penned the biting verse :
'All things are laughter, all things shadow be,
And all things nothing are, and vanity.'
Then why these tears, and why this senseless sorrow,
This loud-voiced dirge that rends the air with discord?

It is enough : a long farewell to tears ;
Or woman let it be alone who weeps :
'Tis ours to crown his obsequies with singing,
And scatter on his tomb Hyblæan roses,
And garlands from Hymettus—all fair flowers,
And to fair flowers to add the feeling song.
Here rest his bones : his soul ascends to heaven :
Traveller, pass on: Reader, nought here asks tears:
Smith has exchanged a happy lot below
For one far happier in the realms above :
And now fulfilled with God, he walks the stars.
The hidden snares of men he there despises,
The daily din and midnight treachery,
The secret plots, and desperate attempts,
The cruel ire and thunderbolts of Kings,
The wheel of Fortune and the shocks of War.

GABRIEL HARVEY,
Epilogue on Sir T. Smith, 1578.

Tears

AND were it for thy profit, to obtain
All sunshine? No vicissitude of rain?
Think'st thou, that thy laborious plough requires
Not Winter frosts, as well as Summer fires?
There must be both: sometimes these hearts of ours
Must have the sweet, the seasonable showers

Of teares : sometimes the frost of chill despaire
Makes our desired sunshine seem more faire :
Weathers that most oppose to flesh and blood,
Are such as help to make our Harvest good :
We may not choose, great God : it is thy task :
We known not what to have, nor how to ask.

F. QUARLES, *Divine Fancies*, 1632.

Ease of Mind

IF the power of art can draw
Nature from her first election,
To a more refinëd lawe
By extracting her perfection ;

Let it now breathe its perfume,
And with slumber strike the braine ;
Now your greatest strength assume,
Run through euerie nerue and vaine.

Lett a silent wonder ceaze
All his thoughts that hee may find,
There is artificiall ease
For the troubles of the mind :
And if thou dost sett him free,
Nature then will yield to thee.

ARTHUR WILSON, *The Inconstant Ladie*, 1646.

Aspiration

SINCE, then, the soul is circumscrib'd within
The narrow limits of a tender skin
Let us be babes in innocence, and grow
Strong upwards, and more weak to things below.
By sacred chymistrie, the spirit must
Ascend and leave the sediment to dust.

ARTHUR WILSON, *To Edward Benlowes*, 1652.

Hope

On the Virtues

HOPE, child, to-morrow, and to-morrow still,
And every morrow hope ; trust while you live.
Hope ! and each time the dawn doth heaven fill,
Be there to ask, as God is there to give.

Poor angel ! Say, 'For sin is sorrow sent ;
Perchance, if long I weep on bended knee,
When He has first blessed all the Innocent,
Then all the Contrite, God may end with me.'

HENRY CARRINGTON, (translated),
Anthology of French Poetry.

O THOU who clingest still to life and love,
Though nought of good, no God thou may'st discern,
Though nought that is, thine utmost woe can move,
Though no soul knows wherewith thine heart doth yearn,
Yet, since thy weary lips no curse can learn,
Cast no least thing thou lovedst once away,
Since yet perchance thine eyes shall see the day.

WILLIAM MORRIS, *The Earthly Paradise.*

Self-government

IF none other thing were required in a faythfull enstructor but onely that he should teach his schollers grammer, or such other sciences, then with lesser travaile might wee attayne unto perfection, sythens grammar and all the liberal Sciences are by traditions left unto us in such sort that, without any greate difficultie, the doubt thereof may be resolved; but the Schoole Master which careth for none other thing but onely to make his schollers lerned, may in some respect be compared to the horsecourser, which onelie careth to feede his horse fat, and never delighteth to ryde him, manage him, or make him handsome; and when such palfryes come to jorneying, they are comonly so provander-proude, that they praunce at the fyrst exceedingly, but being put to a long journey or service, they melt their owne greace, and are not able to endure travaile. Even so, ye mindes of yong men, being onely trained in knowledge of arts, and never perswaded in points of moral reformation, become oftentimes so prowde and so headie that they are carried away with a vaine imagination of their own excellencie. . . . For the mind of man is so heavenlie a thing, and of such rare excellencie, that it alwaies worketh, and can not be idle. And if with the quickness of conceyt it be tempred by a modest moderation, to have regard unto vertue and moralitie, then proveth it both goodly & godly; whereas if it on hedlong, only led by natural considerations of causes, it may prove admirable for some passing quallitie, but it seldome is seene commendable, or allowed for perfection.

George Gascoigne,
The Glasse of Government, 1575.

Self-knowledge

O MIND the secret sprigs and tender plants. Now you are called to dress the garden. Let not the weeds and wild plants remain. Peevishness is a weed: anger is a weed; self-love and self-will are weeds; pride is a wild plant; carelessness is a wild plant; lightness and vanity are wild plants ; and lust is the root of all. And these things have had a room in your gardens, and have been tall and strong ; and truth, innocency and equity have been left out and could not be found, until the Sun of Righteousness arose and searched out that which was lost. Therefore stand not idle, but come into the vineyard and work.

JAMES PARNELL, 1656.

HOW poor a thing is man ! How vain's his mind !
How strange ! how base, and wavering like the wind.
How uncouth are his ways. How full of danger.
How to himself is he himself a stranger.

QUARLES, *Feast for Worms*, 1642.

EVEN as the soyle (which April's showers
Have filled with sweetness, and enricht with flowers),
Reares up her suckling plants, still shooting forth
The tender blossoms of her timely birth ;
But, if denied the beames of cheery May,
They hang their withered heads and fade away :
So man, assisted by th' Almightie's hand,
His faith doth flourish and securely stand,
But, left awhile, forsooke (as in a shade),
It languishes, and, nipt with sin, doth fade.

QUARLES, *Job Militant*.

WE to ourselves most partial judges be,
And faults in others, not ourselves, can see,
Our enemies we fain would have 'em haltered
But when we judge ourselves the case is altered.

W. WINSTANLEY, *The New Help to Discourse*.

On Going to Church

On the Virtues

NO matter whether (some there be that say)
Or goe to church, or stay at home, if pray:
Smith's dainty Sermons have, in plenty, stor'd me,
With better stuffe, than Pulpits can afford me;
Tell me, why pray'st thou? Heaven commanded so;
Art not commanded to his Temples too?
Small store of manners! when thy Prince bids come
And feast at Court: to say, I've meat at home.

F. QUARLES, *Divine Fancies.*

Invention

AND, therefore, I do earnestly exhort those that are young, especially Gentlemen, to set upon these studies, and take some pains in them. They may possibly invent something of eminent use and advantage to the World; and one such discovery would abundantly compensate the Expence and Travel of one Man's whole Life. However, it is enough to maintain and continue what is already invented, neither do I see what more ingenious and manly Employment they can pursue, lending more to the satisfaction of their own minds, and the illustration of the glory of God, for He is wonderful in all His works. But I would not have any Man cross his natural Genius or Inclinations, or undertake such Methods of Study, as his Parts are not fitted to, or not serve those ends to which his Friends, upon mature deliberation, have designed him; but those who do abound with leisure, or who have a natural Propension and Genius inclining them thereto; or those who by reason of the Strength and Greatness of their Parts, are able to compass and comprehend the whole Latitude of Learning.

JOHN RAY, *The Wisdom of God in the Creation.*

Fitness

LET thy apparell be decent, and suited to the quality of thy place and purse. Too much punctualitie, and too much morositie, are the two poles of pride. Be neither too early in the fashion, or too long out of it, nor too precisely in it. What custome hath civiliz'd is become decent; till then, ridiculous; where the eye is the jury, thy apparell is the evidence.

Bring thy daughter a husband of her own religion, and of no hereditary disease. Let his wisdom outweigh his wealth. Let his parentage excell his person, and let his yeares exceed hers. Let thy prayers recommend the rest to Providence. If he prove, thou hast found a sonne, if not, thou hast lost a daughter.

QUARLES, *Enchiridion.*

Courage

I HAVE often been asked if I was nervous the first time I came under fire, and I have always answered truthfully, 'Yes,' although I cannot say that my statement has always been credited. Not only was I nervous the first time, but throughout my service, the first shot in every action, passing near me, has been acutely felt, unless I had some duty on hand at the moment.

The sense of duty preoccupies a man, and not only from what I felt, but from what I have seen in many actions, the strain on the nerves of a gun detachment is considerably lessened by the fact that the service of a gun being dependent on combined action, compels a gunner to concentrate his thoughts on his work. I believe Generals, or any officers in command, who have responsibility, if they are the right sort, lose all sense of personal fear. At the end of the first bombardment, which lasted a week, I was conscious of a decided feeling of exultation in the presence of danger, such as men feel when they do well in manly sports, or women when they realise they are pre-eminent among their compeers.

Sir Evelyn Wood,
From Midshipman to Field Marshal, 1906.

Daring

THERE is at least nothing dishonourable in holding one's life cheap, however small the stake played for; whilst in an age of self-advertisement some tolerance ought to be extended to one who makes himself known by courting danger, whether in earth, sea or sky. . . . However, there is a wide difference between risking your life through pure ignorance of its value and shunning danger when by so doing you must soil the escutcheon of bravery, which should be the most precious possession of every good Englishman. Indifference to danger in a good cause, and especially where a man's honour is at stake, is absolutely essential. . . . For myself I must go further, and declare that it is necessary, unless we are to perish like the Romans in the lap of peace and luxury, that some of us should strive to keep alive the reputation which Englishmen have always had of greatly daring and suffering all things. Surely where there is a daring deed to be done in any part of the world, an Englishman should leap to the front to accomplish it.

On Daring

SIR CLAUDE CHAMPION DE CRESPIGNY.

Forty Years of a Sportsman's Life, 1910.

ON WOMAN, LIFE, AND THE ART OF LIVING

Of all qualities a woman must not have one qualitie of a ship, and that is, too much rigging. A world of wonders it is, to see a woman created in God's image, so miscreate oft times and deformed, with her French, her Spanish, and her foolish fashions, that He that made her, when He looks upon her, shall hardly know her, with her plumes, her fannes, and a silken vizard, with a ruffe like a saile, yea, a ruffe like a rainebow, with a feather in her cap like a flag in her top, to tell (I thinke) which way the wind will blow. . . But what saith the Scripture? *The King's daughter is all glorious within.* (Psalm xlv.), and as ships which are the fairest in shew, yet are not alwayes the fittest for use, so neither are women the more to bee esteemed, but the more to be suspected for their faire trappings.

A Wedding Sermon, 1607.

The figure of this world I can compare
To garden plots, and such like pleasaunt places.
The world breedes men of sundry shape and share,
As hearbes in gardens grow of sundry graces:
Some good, some bad, some amiable faces,
Some foule, some gentle, some of froward mind,
Subject, like bloome, to blast of every wind.

If thou sitte here to viewe this pleasant garden place,
Think thus: at last will come a frost, and all these floures deface:
But if thou sitte at ease to rest thy wearie bones,
Remember death brings finall rest to all oure greeuous grones.
So whether for delight, or here thou sitte, for ease,
Think still upon the latter day, as shalt thou God best please.

George Gascoigne.

Written at the end of a close walk in his garden, Walthamstow, 1575.

To Golden Hair

AH, Pyrrha, tell me, whose the happy lot
To woo thee on a couch of lavish roses,
Who, bathed in odorous dews, in his fond arm encloses
Thee, in some happy grot?

For whom those nets of golden-gloried hair
Dost thou entwine in cunning carelessnesses?
Alas, poor boy! who thee, in fond belief, caresses,
Deeming thee wholly fair!

How oft shall he thy fickleness bemoan,
When fair to foul shall change; and he unskilful
In pilotage, beholds, with tempest wildly wilful,
The happy calm o'erthrown!

He who now hopes that thou wilt ever prove
All void of care, and full of fond endearing,
Knows not that varies more than Zephyrs ever-veering,
The fickle breath of love.

Ah, hapless he to whom, like seas untried,
Thou seemest fair! That my sea-going's ended
My votive tablet proves, to those dark gods suspended
Who o'er the waves preside.

TOM HOOD.

S. A. COURTAULD'S *Selected Metrical Translations of the Odes of Horace*, 1909.

Inconstant Woman

On Woman

THE ill woman is inconstant, light-headed and vaine ; now she loves, anon she hates, now she obeyes, anon she rebels ; gentle and kinde to-day, crooked and unkinde to-morrow ; for she sailes but by gusts, and all her goodnesse takes her by fits, like the good daies of an ague.

J. COLBY, *The Scarcity and Excellency of Virtuous Women*, 1710.

Flee and she follows ; follow and she'll flee.
Than she there's none more coy ; there's none more fond than she.

QUARLES, *Emblems*.

AS when a *Lady* (walking Flora's Bowre)
Picks here a pinke, and there a gilly-flowre,
Now plucks a vi'let from her purple bed,
And then a primrose (the yeare's maiden-head)
There nips the bryer ; here, the Lovers Pancey.
Shifting her dainty pleasures with her Fancy ;
This, on her arms ; and that she lifts to weare
Upon the borders of her curious haire ;
At length, a Rose-bud (passing all the rest)
She plucks, and bosomes in her Lilly brest.

QUARLES, *Queen Esther*.

Her Proper Sphere

A WOMAN'S rule should be in such a fashion,
Only to guide her household, and her passion :
And her obedience never's out of season
So long as either Husband lasts, or Reason :

Ill thrives the hapless Family, that showes
A Cock that 's silent, and a Hen that crows :
I know not which live more ungodly lives,
Obeying Husbands, or commanding Wives.

QUARLES, *Queen Esther.*

A Man's Modesty

To the most choice Gentlewoman, and ornament of her sexe, Mrs. Elizabeth Goode, daughter of Sebastian Goode, Esquire, at Maldon.

MRS. ELIZABETH,

I HAVE long beene an earnest suitor to your honour and deserts, that I might be admitted an humble suitor to your sweet selfe. . . . . Amongst all the works of God, I delight most in beholdinge (the sun excepted) an amiable countenance ; and such is yours, or none in these parts of England. Your face is a mappe of beauties, your gentle breast a cabinett of vertues, and your whole selfe a cluster of all the choicest delicacies : but, in plaine English, not your pleasinge aspect, nor well-featured person, nor admired excellencies, nor weighty portion, fastened my affections on you, but your love (of this I have beene long persuaded) to a man (myself, I mean) so undeserving it. As for myselfe, I am thought worthy of a good wife, though unworthy of you. These pretty toyes, called husbands, are such rare commodities in this age, that I can woo and winne wives by the dozen. I knowe not any gentlewoman in these parts, but would kisse a letter from my hands, read it with joye, and then laye it up next her hart as a treasure; but I will not trye their courtesies, except I find you discourteous. . . . Lay your hand upon your hart, and resolve to say Amen to my desires. If so, I shall accept your portion with the left hand and your lovely person with the right. . . .

Your most hearty Friend and Servant,

2 Dec., 1644. THOMAS BOURMAN.

'The Tobacconist'

THERE were two maids talking of husbands, which is for the most part the theme of their discourse, and the subject of their thoughts.

The one said: I would not marry a man that takes tobacco, for anything.

Then, said the other, It is likely you will have a fool for your husband; for tobacco is able to make a fool a wise man: and though it doth not always work wise effects, by reason some fools are beyond all improvement yet it never fails where any improvement is to be made.

Why, said the first, What wise effects does it work?

The second said: It composes the mind, it busies the thoughts, represents several objects to the mind's view, settles and stays the senses, clears the understanding, strengthens the judgment, spies out errors, evaporates follies, heals ambition, comforts sorrow, abates passions, excites to noble actions, digests conception, enlarges knowledge, elevates imaginations, creates fancies, quickens wit, and makes reason pleader and truth judge in all disputes or controversies betwixt right and wrong.

The first said: It makes the breath stink.

You mistake, said the second, it will make a stinking breath sweet.

It is a beastly smell, said the first.

Said the second: Civet is a beastly smell, and that you will thrust your nose to, although it be an excrement; and for anything we know, so is ambergreece; when tobacco is a sweet and pleasant, wholesome and medicinal herb.

MARGARET, DUCHESS OF NEWCASTLE,
Feigned Stories in Prose, 1656.

Man's Place in Creation

MAN is Heaven's masterpiece.

How can I mend my title then? Where can
Ambition find a higher style than man?

F. QUARLES.

The Span of Life

ASK not. 'Twere impious to know,
Nor mystic numbers search, to see
What term of years the gods bestow
On thee or me, Leuconoë.

Take what is sent, 'tis Jove decrees
If yet more winters be in store;
Or this our last, whose billowy seas
Beat on the worn Tyrrhenian shore.

Then strain thy wines, my friend, be wise;
No shadowy hopes the hours can stay:
E'en while we speak, time envious flies—
Trust not to-morrow, live to-day!

GEORGE COURTAULD,
From *Horace*, Book I., Ode xi.

What is Your Life ?

On Life

LIKE to the Damask Rose you see,
Or like the blossome on the tree,
Or like the dainty flower of May ;
Or like the morning to the day ;
Or like the Sun, or like the shade ;
Or like the Gourd which Jonas had ;
Even such is man, whose thread is spun,
Drawn out, and cut, and so is done.

The Rose withers, the blossome blasteth ;
The Flower fades, the morning hasteth :
The Sun sets, the shadow flies,
The Gourd consumes, and man he dies.

Like to the blaze of fond delight ;
Or like the morning cleare and bright ;
Or like a frost ; or like a shower ;
Or like the pride of Babel's tower ;
Or like the hour that guides the Time ;
Or like the beauty in her prime ;
Even such is man, whose glory lends
His life a blaze or two, and ends.

Delights vanish, the morn o'er-casteth ;
The frost breaks, the shower hasteth ;
The tower falls, the hour spends ;
The beauty fades, and man's life ends.

QUARLES, *Argalus and Parthenia*, 1629.

MAN'S life is fickle, full of wingëd haste,
It mocks the sense with joy, and soon doth waste.
Pleasure does crown thy youth, and lulls thy wants ;
But (sullen age approaching) straight avaunts.
Man's life is joy, and sorrow seeks to banish,
It doth lament and mourn in age, and vanish.

The time of pleasure 's like the life of Man ;
Both joyful, both containëd in a span ;
Both highly priz'd, and both on sudden lost,
When most we trust them, they deceive us most.
What fit of madness makes us love them thus ?
We leave our lives, and pleasure leaveth us :
Why, what are pleasures ? But a golden dream,
Which (waking) makes our wants the more extreme ?
And what is Life ? A bubble full of care,
Which (prickt by death) straight empties into air :
The flowers (clad in far more rich array,
Than e'er was Solomon) doe soone decay ;
What thing more sweet, or fairer than a flower ?
And yet it blooms and fades within an hour ;
What greater pleasure than a morning Sun ?
And yet this pleasure every day is dun.

QUARLES, *A Feast for Worms.*

Live for Others

NO man is born unto himself alone :
Who lives unto himself, he lives to none.
The world's a body, each man a member is,
To add some measure to the public blisse.
Beasts only breathe ; 'tis man alone doth live ;
The end of man's creation was society,
Mutual Communion, and friendly Piety ;
The man that lives unto himselfe alone,
Subsists and breathes, but lives not. Never one
Deserv'd the moiety of himselfe, for he
That 's borne, may challenge but one part of three ;
Triparted thus ; his Country claims the best ;
The next, his Parents ; and himselfe the least.
He husbands best his life, that freely gives
It for the public good. He rightly lives.

QUARLES, *Esther.*

Character

The Art of Living

ALL Arts are but the supply of Nature's defects, to patch up her ragged and worne rents, to cover rather than to cure or recover Man's fall; even that King of Arts, the Politicall Art of Kings, is not heire by whole bloud; but the gift of God, begotten since the fall, and abundantly argues our unrulinesse otherwise, which must have Lords and Lawes to rule us.

SAMUEL PURCHAS, *His Pilgrims*, 1625.

Men are known by little things, by the incidents of the day, better than they can be by more prominent and important events.

STEPHEN MORELL, *Excursions of Virgilius*.

A man, like a watch, is to be valued for his going.

He that prefers him on other accounts, bows to an Idol.

Unless Virtue guides us, our choice must be wrong.

An able, bad man is an ill Instrument, and to be shunned as the Plague.

Be not deceived with the first appearance of things, but give thyself Time to be in the right.

Show is not Substance: Realities govern wise Men.

Have a care, therefore, where there is more Sail than Ballast.

WILLIAM PENN, *Some Fruits of Solitude*.

Meditations

I

Upon taking a great deal of pains to take a spot of ink out of a white paper, yet some sully still remaining.

The Art of Living

HOW much pains have I taken to take out this spot, and yet, though I have, by the help of the knife, taken away the blackness, yet all the rubbing I can do will not so quite take away the spot, but that something will remain that discovers it was once there; which makes me, in my thoughts, compare this blot in the white paper to that in one's reputation; which, when it has been once blurred by the vulgar's voice, though ever so much pain has been taken to remove and quite take out the spot, yet all has been ineffectual, for though possibly something of the untrue report has been silenced, yet it has still left some blur, and so much sully that it never was quite removed.

II

Upon staying between Chelsea and Leez to bait at Burnt Wood at dinner.

WITH what cheerfulness and serenity of mind did I bear with all the inconveniences and ill entertainment of this inn, upon this consideration that what I met with there was not to last, but at night, when I came home to my own house, I should have abundant recompense made me by the good things I should there enjoy. O, my soul, turn this into spiritual advantage and consider that all the ill entertainment I meet with in this vain world is but the ill accommodations of this great Inn; and when thou hast past through this howling wilderness and hast finished thy great journey, thou shalt come to Heaven to thy home where, when thou hast been but one hour, it will make thee forget all troubles thou meetest with in the way.

MARY RICH (Countess of Warwick), 1667.

The Arts of Speech

BEWARE of him that is slow to anger: anger when it is long in coming, is the strongest when it comes, and the longer kept. Abused patience turns to fury; when fancy is the ground of passion, that understanding which composes the fancy, qualifies the passion; but when judgement is the ground, the memory is the Recorder.

Give not thy tongue too great a liberty, lest it take thee prisoner. A word unspoken is like the sword in thy scabbard, thine; if vented, the sword is in another's hand. If thou desire to be held wise, be so wise as to hold thy tongue.

Hath any wounded thee with Injuries? Meet them with patience. Hastie words ranckle the wound, soft language dresses it, forgiveness cures it, and oblivion takes away the scarre. It is more noble, by silence, to avoid an injury, than by argument to overcome it.

In every relative action, change conditions with thy brother. Then ask thy conscience what thou would'st be done to; being truly resolved exchange again, and do thou the like to him, and thy Charity shall never err; it is injustice to do what without impatience thou canst not suffer.

QUARLES, *Enchiridion.*

In matters of difficulty it is best to say as little as possible, but that to the purpose; and not to take up things on too slight grounds, nor be hasty to judge without weighing circumstances and cases; ever keeping in view the Judge of all.

MRS. ELIZABETH TAYLOR, *Memoir*, 1849.

Of Good Manners

GENTLEMEN will gently doe where gentlenes is shewed.

THOMAS TUSSER,
Five Hundred Points of Good Husbandrie.

Every Action done in the World ought to be done with some Sign of Respect to those that are present.

At Play, and at Fire, 'tis good Manners to give place to the last comer.

Reproach none for the Infirmities of Nature, nor delight to put them that have them in mind thereof.

Show not yourself Glad at the Misfortune of another, tho' he were your Enemy.

When a Man does all he can, though it succeeds not well, blame not him that did it.

Take all Admonitions thankfully, in what Time or Place soever given; but afterwards, not being faulty, take Time and Place convenient, with Modesty, to let him know it that gave them.

Be not too hasty to believe flying Reports, to the Disparagement of any.

Be modest in Apparel, and endeavour to accommodate Nature, rather than to procure Admiration.

Undertake not what you cannot perform; but be careful to keep your Promise.

Contradict not, at every Turn, what others say, so as to contend and say, *It is not so: it is as I say.* But rather comply, especially in things of small Consequence.

Associate yourself with Men of good Quality, if you esteem your own reputation; for 'tis better to be alone than in bad company.

Laugh not much, or loud, at any public Spectacle.

Let your Discourse which you make to Men of Business be short.

Undertake not to teach your Equals in the Art they profess; it savours of arrogancy.

Run not in the Streets, neither go too slowly, nor with thy Mouth open; go not shaking your Arms; nor trail your Feet after you; go not upon your Toes, nor in a dancing, capering, tripping manner with your Heels.

Reprehend not the Imperfections of others, for that belongs to Fathers, Masters and Superiors.

Whisper not in the Company of others.

Be not curious to know the Affairs of others, neither approach to those who speak in private.

Speak not evil of the absent, for it is unjust, when the Party is not there to clear himself.

If you would enjoy true Content, live peacefully in that Vocation unto which Providence hath called you.

W. WINSTANLEY, *The New Help to Discourse.*

Use and Abuse of Travel

AS for Gentlemen, Travell is accounted an excellent Ornament to them; and therefore many of them coming to their Lands sooner than to their Wits, adventure themselves to see the Fashions of other Countries, where their soules and bodies find temptations to a twofold Whoredom, whencc they see the World as Adam had knowledge of good and evill, with the losse or lessening of their estate in this English (and perhaps also in the heavenly) Paradise, and bring home a few smattering termes, flattering garbes, apish cringings, foppish fancies, foolish guises and disguises, the vanities of Neighbour Nations (I name not Naples), without furthering of their knowledge of God, the World, or themselves. I speake not against Travell, so usefull to usefull men.

SAMUEL PURCHAS, *His Pilgrimes*, 1625.

BALLADS, SONGS AND RHYMES

A PRETTY THING

Who am I that shine so bright,
With my pretty yellow light,
Peeping through your curtains grey?
Tell me, little girl, I pray.

When the sun is gone, I rise,
In the very silent skies;
And a cloud or two doth skim
Round about my silver rim.

All the little stars do seem,
Hidden by my brighter beam;
And among them I do ride,
Like a queen in all her pride.

Then the reaper goes along,
Singing forth a merry song,
Whilst I light the shaking leaves,
And the yellow harvest sheaves.

Little girl, consider well,
Who this simple tale doth tell;
And I think you'll guess it soon,
For I only am the Moon.

JANE TAYLOR, *Original Poems*

The Death of Brihtnoth

THERE Brihtnoth then arrayed his men and taught them how to stand,
To keep their ranks, and fearless grasp the buckler in the hand.
And when they were in order set, he lighted from his steed,
Among his own loved household—men whom he knew good at need.
The herald of the Vikings stood beside the river shore,
And the sea-rover's haughty words before the Earl he bore:
'From seaman bold I come: they bid that thou shalt straightway send
Treasure for ransom: better 'twill be for you in the end
To buy with gifts our onslaught off than with us war to hold.
No need to fight if ye agree—we'll make a peace for gold:
If so thou orderest it, who here among the rest art chief,
That thou wilt set thy people free, then bid for their relief,
That they shall to the seamen give as seamen shall decree
Treasure for peace; then take ye peace: and we will put to sea
With booty-laden ships, and peace henceforth between us be!'

Then Brihtnoth lifted up his voice—his shield he brandished high,
And shook his slender ashen shaft—and thus he made reply.
Wrathful and resolute he spake: 'O thou sea-robber, hear

What saith this folk! To you they give no tribute but the spear,
The venomed point, the old keen edge, and all the battle gear
That works no good for you in fight! Go, seamen's herald, say
This message of yet deeper hate: that here, an Earl, I stay,
Undaunted with my men to guard the kingdom, folk and land
Of Ethelred, my lord. . . . '
With that he bade his men go forth, their bucklers then they bore,
Till at the landing-place they stood beside the river shore.
Neither could reach the other there—between them flowed the tide;
For after ebb the flood rolled up, it filled the channel wide.
And till their spears together clashed, too long the the time did seem
To Vikings' and East Saxon ranks arrayed by Panta's stream,
For neither could the other hurt, save by the arrow's flight,
Till ebb of tide. . . .

Now drew the time of glorious deeds, the tide of battle nigh:
And now the fatal hour was come when death-doomed men must die!
Now loud uprose the battle-cry, and greedy for their prey,
The ravens wheeled, the eagles screamed, on earth was noise of fray.
From hand was hurled the sharp-filed spear, the whetted arrow flew;
The bow was busy, shield met spear, and fierce the combat grew:

*　　　*　　　*　　　*

On earth was slaughter! Firm they stood; and Brihtnoth's words of flame
Stirred every heart to bide the brunt and win a glorious name.
Forth went the hero old in war, he raised his sheltering shield,
And shook his spear, and onward went into the battle field.

*　　　*　　　*　　　*

For the day's work, he rendered thanks, that God to him had given:
But from a warrior's clenchëd hand a dart was fiercely driven.
Too sure it went, and pierced the noble thane of Ethelred.
Beside him stood a beardless youth—a boy in battle dread—
Young Wulfmær, son of Wulfstau: he swift from the hero drew
The bloody dart and hurled it back: the hardened spear-head flew,
And on the earth the Viking lay who thus had reached his lord.
Then rushed a warrior armed to seize the goodly graven sword,
Bracelets and corslet of the Earl, but Brihtnoth drew his blade,
Brown-edged and broad, and fierce the strokes he on his corselet laid.
Too soon another smote his arm and hindered him. Then rolled
On earth the yellow-hilted sword, no longer could he hold
Keen blade, nor weapon wield; but still the grey-haired leader bade
His men keep heart and onward press, good comrades undismayed.

No longer could he stand upright, his eyes to heaven he bent :
'Ruler of nations ! I give thanks for all that Thou hast lent
Of joys in this world. Now have I, O gracious Lord ! most need
That Thou show favour to my soul, that it to Thee may speed,
And to this kingdom, Lord of Angels ! pass in peace, I pray
That hell-foes do me no despite.' They hewed him as he lay—
The heathen dogs ! and two with him, Ælfnoth and Wulfmœr,
Beside their lord they gave their lives.

The Song of the Battle of Maldon, A.D. 991, translated from the Anglo Saxon by H. W. LUMSDEN, 1887.

Prior and Morley at Down Hall

I SING not old Jason, who Travelled thro' Greece
To Kiss the fair Maids and possess the rich Fleece :
Nor sing I Æneas who led by his Mother,
Got rid of one Wife and went far for another.

But I sing Exploits that have lately been done
By Two British Heroes call'd Matthew and John ;
And how they rid Friendly from fine London town,
Fair Essex to see and a place they called Down.

And thus Matthew said, look you here, my Friend John
I fairly have Travelled Years Thirty and One ;
And tho' I still carry'd my Sovereign's Warrants,
I only have gone upon other Folks' Errands.

And now in this Journey of Life I wou'd have
A Place where to Bait 'twixt the court and the
Grave ;
Where joyful to Live, not unwilling to Die—
Gadzooks, I have just such a Place in my Eye.

There are Gardens so stately, and Arbors so
Thick,
A Portal of Stone, and a Fabrick of Brick.
The Matter next Week shall be all in your Pow'r ;
But the Money, gadzooks, must be Paid in an
Hour.

For things in this World, must by Law be made
certain,
We Both must repair unto Oliver Martin ;
For he is a Lawyer of worldly renown,
I'll bring You to see ; he must fix you at Down.

So to Harlow they came ; and hey, where are
You all ?
Show Us into the Parlor, and mind when I call :
Why your Maids have no motion, your Men have
no life ;
Well, Master, I hear you have Bury'd your Wife.

Come this very instant, take care to provide
Tea, Sugar, and Toast, and a Horse and a Guide.
Are the Harrisons here, both the Old and the
Young ?
And where stands fair Down, the delight of my
song ?

O Squire, to the Grief of my Heart, I may say,
I have buried Two Wives since you travelled this
way ;
And the Harrisons both may be presently here ;
And Down stands, I think, where it stood the last
Year.

Then Joan brought the Tea-pot, and Caleb the Toast;
And the Wine was froth'd out by the Hand of my Host:
But we clear'd our Extempore Banquet so fast,
That the Harrisons both were forgot in the haste.

Now, hey for Down Hall; for the Guide he was got:
The chariot was mounted, the horses did trot;
The Guide he did bring us a Dozen Mile round:
But O! all in vain; for no Down could be found.

O! here I spy Down, cast your Eye to the West,
Where a Windmill so stately stands plainly confest.
On the West, reply'd Matthew, no Windmill I find;
As well Thou may'st tell me, I see the West-wind.

Now, pardon me, Morley, the Windmill I spy;
But, faithful Achates, no House is there nigh.
Look again, says mild Morley, gadzooks, you are blind;
The Mill stands before, and the House lies behind.

O, now a low, ruin'd white shed I discern,
Until'd and unglaz'd; I believe 'tis a Barn.
A Barn! Why, you rave; 'tis a House for a Squire,
A Justice of Peace, or a Knight of our shire!

A house should be Built or with Brick or with Stone.
Why, 'tis Plaster and Lath; and I think that's all One.
And such as it is, it has stood with great Fame,
Been callëd a Hall, and has given its name
To Down, down, hey derry down.

O Morley, O Morley, if that be a Hall ;
The fame with the Building will suddenly fall—
With your friend, Jimmy Gibbs, about Buildings
agree ;
My business is Land ; and it matters not me.

I wish you could tell, what a duce your head ails.
I show'd you Down Hall ; did you look for Ver-
sailles ?
Then take House and Farm, as John Ballet will
let you ;
For better, for worse, as I took my Dame Betty.

And now, Sir, a word to the Wise is enough ;
You 'll make very little of all your Old Stuff :
And to build at your Age, by my Troth, you grow
simple.
Are you Young and Rich, like the Master of
Wimple ?

If you have these whims of Apartments and
Gardens,
From Twice Fifty Acres you 'll ne'er see five
farthings,
And in Yours I shall find the true Gentleman's
Fate :
E'er you finish your House, you 'll have spent your
Estate.

Now let Us touch Thumbs, and be Friends ere
we part :
Here, John, is my Thumb, and here, Matt, is my
Heart.
To Halstead I speed ; and you go back to Town.
Thus ends the first part of the Ballad of Down.
Derry down, down, hey derry down.

MATTHEW PRIOR, *Ballad of Down Hall*, (1720).

The Village Church
(*Little Canfield*)

THE Porch's richly panelled wall,
Unfolds an arched and shafted way,
Which, like the heav'nly gate, to all
Gives access ever in the day.
Through the open side-lights oft the ray
Of sunshine speeds with gladden'd look,
And small birds hie for rest or play,
Familiar with each coign and nook.

Ere through the Norman door we pass,
Note well the structure, plain and old,
The time-worn stone, the oaken mass
With iron hinge of graceful mould.
Outside it, sleeps the world so cold!
Inside, O what awakening lore
Reminds us oft of Him Who told
His faithful flock, 'I am the door!'

* * * *

Advance we through the central aisle
Where seats unbarred by doors expand;
Pass we where wrought in ruder style
The reading desk and pulpit stand:
Then mark the screen by which is spann'd
The Chancel-arch, how dark and old!
Carv'd out of oak by cunning hand
With pointed tracery rich and bold.

Close to the window, quaintly nich'd,
An old Piscina decks the wall,
With foliate head not unenrich'd,
Nor meanly moulded, though but small.
The hole through which the Priest let fall
The water which had cleaned his hands,
Or rins'd the holy vessels all,
For the Lord's Supper still expands.

*   *   *   *

Carv'd in the chancel's northern wall,
  In precinct hallow'd and retir'd
And like a mural tomb (though small,
  Were space for effigy requir'd),
A niche recedes, with roof admir'd
  For flowery pendent, moulded groin,
And all of grace which love untir'd
  Could throw on panel, shaft and coign.

*   *   *   *

Pierc'd through the wall, near this, a stair
  Winds upward to the Vestry floor,
Where lie preserv'd with reverent care
  The records of parochial lore :
Most quaint are those from days of yore
  Matching yon aged wooden chest
With triple lock, which heretofore
  Held holy plate and priestly vest.

*   *   *   *

Within the porch on either side,
  A bench of stone invites repose,
After long walk in summer-tide,
  Until 'the Parson's ring' shall close :
And old men seated on the rows
  Ask of each other how they fare,
Discoursing, while the zephyr blows
  And gently lifts their silver hair.

The bell is hush'd. Sedately now
  All enter, and as up the aisle
Each old man moves, he makes his bow
  Towards the Priest in the olden style :
Nor let the modern sceptic smile
  At usage so remote and dim ;
God sees there homage without guile,
  And reckons it as paid to Him.

C. Lesingham Smith, *Footprints, &c.*, 1868.

The Squire's Pew

A SLANTING ray of evening light
Shoots through the yellow pane;
It makes the faded crimson bright,
And gilds the fringe again:
The window's Gothic frame-work falls
In oblique shadow on the walls.

And since these trappings first were new,
How many a cloudless day,
To rob the velvet of its hue,
Has come and pass'd away!
How many a setting sun hath made
That curious lattice-work of shade!

Crumbled beneath the hillock green
The cunning hand must be,
That carved this fretted door, I ween,
Acorn and fleur-de-lis,
And now the worm hath done her part
In mimicking the chisel's art.

In days of yore (that now we call)
When James the First was king,
The courtly knight from yonder hall
His train did hither bring;
All seated round in order due
With broider'd suit and buckled shoe.

On damask cushions, set in fringe,
All reverently they knelt:
Prayer books with brazen hasp and hinge,
In ancient English spelt,
Each holding in a lily hand,
Responsive at the priest's command.

Now, streaming down the vaulted aisle,
The sunbeam, long and lone,

Illumes the characters awhile
  Of their inscription stone ;
And there, in marble hard and cold,
The Knight and all his train behold.

Outstretch'd together, are express'd
  He and my lady fair,
With hands uplifted on the breast,
  In attitude of prayer ;
Long visag'd, clad in armour, he—
With ruffled arm and bodice, she.

Set forth in order as they died,
  The numerous offspring bend ;
Devoutly kneeling side by side,
  As though they did intend
For past omissions to atone,
By sending endless prayers in stone.

Those mellow days are past and dim,
  But generations new,
In regular descent from him,
  Have fill'd the stately pew ;
And in the same succession, go
To occupy the vault below.

And now the polish'd modern squire
  And his gay train appear,
Who duly to the hall retire,
  A season, every year—
And fill the seats with belle and beau,
As 'twas so many years ago.

Perchance all thoughtless as they tread
  The hollow-sounding floor,
Of that dark house of kindred dead,
  Which shall, as heretofore,
In turn, receive, to silent rest,
Another and another guest.

The feather'd hearse and sable train,
  In all its wonted state,
Shall wind along the village lane,
  And stand before the gate,
Brought many a distant county through
To join the final rendezvous.

And when the race is swept away
  All to their dusty beds,
Still shall the mellow evening ray
  Shine gaily o'er their heads;
While other faces, fresh and new,
Shall occupy the Squire's Pew.

JANE TAYLOR, *Original Poems.*

My Mother

WHO fed me from her gentle breast,
And hushed me in her arms to rest,
And on my cheek sweet kisses prest?
  My Mother.

When sleep forsook my open eye,
Who was it sung sweet lullaby,
And rocked me that I should not cry?
  My Mother.

Who sat and watched my infant head,
When sleeping on my cradle bed,
And tears of sweet affection shed?
  My Mother.

When pain and sickness made me cry,
Who gazed upon my heavy eye,
And wept for fear that I should die?
  My Mother.

Who dressed my doll in clothes so gay,
And taught me pretty how to play,
And minded all I had to say?
  My Mother.

Who ran to help me when I fell,
And would some pretty story tell,
Or kiss the place to make it well?
My Mother.

Who taught my infant lips to pray,
And love God's holy book and day,
And walk in wisdom's pleasant way?
My Mother.

And can I ever cease to be
Affectionate and kind to thee,
Who was so very kind to me,
My Mother?

Ah! no, the thought I cannot bear,
And if God please my life to spare,
I hope I shall reward thy care,
My Mother.

When thou art feeble, old, and grey,
My healthy arm shall be thy stay,
And I will soothe thy pain away,
My Mother.

And when I see thee hang thy head,
'Twill be my turn to watch thy bed,
And tears of sweet affection shed,
My Mother.

ANN TAYLOR, *Original Poems.*

The Danbury Swallow

WHERE Essex lifts her greenest bower,
And shrines an old chief Pastor's love,
Where every leaf on ivied tower
Hears all day long the brooding dove:

From out the crowded haunts of life,
    Now youth, now age comes seeking there
Peace from the battle and the strife,
    As in some fane of restful prayer.

Uncounted leagues of land and sea
    Bring every summer bird that sings.
Each domesday oak, each clovered lea
    Sees all the glancing of their wings.

The tangled brakes of flowering May
    Pass into garlands rosy red ;
And pools of water hold the day,
    Redoubling glories overhead.

The gleaming fisher of the lake
    Sits watching on her shadowed bough ;
Rich turquoise worn for some dear sake
    Set on a dark and lovely brow,

Would pale before the fulgent ray
    That marks the Halcyon's gliding track ;
No mirrored pool beneath her way
    Can throw one half her glories back.

And when she darts upon her prey,
    She darts as with a meteor's flight,
Halo'd in showers of diamond spray,
    Blue flashing in her jewelled light.

And one familiar bird there came,
    That ever sounds her twittering note
By cottage eave and latticed frame,
    From creamy breast and russet throat.

O'er half the world she finds her way
    To skim each year this English lawn ;
Her flight is part of summer day,
    Her wings are busy with the dawn.

She loves no solitary place,
    Nor forest lands, nor moor, nor fen,
She moveth ever in the face,
    And round the meadowed homes of men.

One year, for nest, she chose instead
    Of barn, or eave, or raftered door,
The lowly vestibule that led
    Unto a little chapel floor.

All that fair week she carried straws,
    And built her fragile house with clay:
No hand enforced the household laws
    That would have stopped her happy way.

Next year she came, and flew around,
    On one bright morn of perfect calm;
Her place was echoing to the sound
    Of children's chanting of a psalm.

She sat entranced, and heard the praise
    That David sang of homing bird;
She heard her name from ancient days,
    And wondered at the gracious word.

Then, waiting till the parting few
    Had passed into the blossomed air;
On to God's altar straight she flew,
    And laid her young ones there.

DUKE OF ARGYLL,
The Burdens of Belief, &c., 1894.

Waltham Abbey Bells

THE famous Christmas stanzas of 'In Memoriam' were written on the 'new and unhallowed ground' at High Beech, Epping Forest, and the 'single church below the hill' was Waltham Abbey church.

The time draws near the birth of Christ ;
  The moon is hid, the night is still ;
  The Christmas bells from hill to hill
Answer each other in the night.

Four voices of four hamlets round,
  From far and near, on mead and moor,
  Swell out and fail, as if a door
Were shut between me and the sound.

Each voice four changes on the wind,
  That now dilate and now decrease ;
  Peace and goodwill, goodwill and peace,
Peace and goodwill to all mankind.

*   *   *   *

The time draws near the birth of Christ ;
  The moon is hid, the night is still ;
  A single church below the hill
Is pealing, folded in the mist.

A single peal of bells below
  That wakens at this hour of rest
  A single murmur in the breast,
That these are not the bells I know.

Like strangers' voices here they sound,
  In lands where not a memory strays,
  Nor landmark breathes of other days,
But all is new unhallow'd ground.

*   *   *   *

Ring out, wild bells, to the wild sky,
  The flying cloud, the frosty light :
  The year is dying in the night ;
Ring out, wild bells, and let him die.

Ring out the old, ring in the new,
  Ring, happy bells, across the snow :
  The year is going, let him go ;
Ring out the false, ring in the true.

ALFRED LORD TENNYSON. (1850).

Private Theatricals

Before the curtain rises

THE guests assemble. Down the stairs I
steal,
As if I'd dressed a century before,
And pause, a courtly beau from head to heel,
Close by the green-room door.

The fire-light glows within ; the leaping blaze
Shines on an eager face—what happy spell
Summoned that sweetest glimpse of olden days,
That arch and radiant belle ?

Ready to play her part in quaint disguise
Of powdered hair and old brocaded gown,
She warms a dainty foot, nor turns her eyes
Where, with an anxious frown,

Conning his book, our crafty Villain sits ;
Tall, handsome, honest, he's a wealthy squire—
A trifle heavy—in our telling bits
He rather misses fire.

I push the door, and meet a smile from each ;
My lady's eyes are lifted from the flame ;
The Villain keeps his finger on a sheet,
And greets me by my name.

I am the happy hero of the play,
With Love, and Luck, and Valour on my side ;
I am to conquer everything to-day,
I am to win my bride.

And I will win her ! Ah, they do not know—
Well may they praise me as I act my part !
This courtship of a hundred years ago
Is living in my heart.

Yet I can plead my cause without the aid
Of studied phrases—they are poor and weak ;
Wait only till our comedy is played—
This is no time to speak.

The actors hurry in, and one and all
Appeal to me to listen or to look.
The footman's livery is a size too small,
The prompter wants his book.

My father comes to show his wrinkled face,
And loiters nervously behind the scenes ;
I praise his baldness and his feeble pace,—
He's only in his teens !

There are so many duties to perform,
And at a moment's notice I must say
Who is to see about the thunder-storm,
And who takes in the tray.

Where is the fatal deed that must be signed ?
I give them all their answers, and by chance,
Lounging beside the window, lift the blind
And cast a careless glance.

Nothing to see—how heavily it rains !—
Nothing but here and there a gliding spark,
Where carriages along the country lanes
Come rolling through the dark.

Beyond, there lies a world of gloom unknown ;
Our little space of glitter, warmth and light
Is but a many-coloured bubble, blown
On a black sea of night.

Well, let the bubble break without a sigh,
And let to-morrow come, as come it will ;
I am the happy hero till I die,
If she is with me still !

And when hereafter we recall this day
Of painted, powdered courtship from the past,
We'll laugh at stage and prompter, while I play
The lover to the last !

After the curtain falls.

All's over now. It was a great success.
Our honest Villain did the best he could ;
Took pains and plodded through his wickedness—
He's really very good.

And when he drove the lady to despair
With darkly scowling threats and feigned alarms,
I rushed upon the stage, defied him there,
And clasped her in my arms !

An explanation followed. I embrace
A few relations, quite unknown till then ;
Virtue was lucky, Villainy disgraced—
We all were better men.

Then came my wrinkled sire—'Nay, I mistook,—
You won't bear malice for a blunder—zounds !
Take your old father's gift—a pocket-book,'—
'Twas twenty thousand pounds.

'Bless you, my children ! she's a pearl, my boy!'
The others gathered round for their farewell,
And stood in attitudes, and wished us joy,
And so the curtain fell.

They called us back. The laughing plaudits swelled
To welcome us. That moment was divine—
The token of my triumph ! As I held
My darling's hand in mine.

I seemed to feel her happy pulses beat,
  As mine were beating in my joy and pride;
I trod the whole world underneath my feet
  Since she was by my side!

And then—why, as we passed, I overheard
  A hurried whisper, caught a meaning smile:
Enough—it was the Villain she preferred—
  The Villain all the while!

That was the end, and here I am alone
  Dismally laughing at my sorry plight;
I listen to the wind's unceasing moan,
  I gaze into the night.

Only to see my pale reflection cast
  Upon the gloom. A bitter lash of rain
Falls, with a sudden fury of the blast,
  On the black window pane.

She loves him—loves him! She will be his wife!
  And strangely I recall, as here I stand,
How in another world, another life,
  I bowed, and dropped her hand.

What did I think of, as I bent my head?
  The fire-light flashed upon my buckled shoes—
Poor hero! Well, there's nothing to be said—
  Was she not free to choose?

She did not know! With my whole heart I played.
  What then? She thought I acted well, no doubt;
If Love came stealing through the masquerade,
  How should she find him out?

She did not know! God bless her in her choice!
  (Ay, and the Villain too!) No thought of blame
Shall ever lend its hardness to my voice
  When I would speak her name.

There will be other plays in coming years
  When this is half forgotten ; there will be
New scenes, new dresses, and new hopes and fears,
  But this old play for me !

One can't be always learning things by heart ;
  Variety is charming—yet it palls.
'Zounds !'—(as the father said)—I'll play my part
  Until the curtain falls.

MARGARET VELEY, *A Marriage of Shadows*, 1888.

The Passing of Summer

ABOVE, the sky was blue, and all around
  The scent of flowers was heavy on the air ;
Through all the land joy seemed in every sound,
  And all was peace : Summer reigned everywhere.

She sat upon a bank, all strewn with flowers,
  Attended by her maidens, June, July,
And August, who to light the passing hours,
  In turn brought stores of flowers of richest dye.

Above her hung cascades of 'golden rain,'
  Left there by one of Spring's attendants, May,
To shield her from the sun that tried in vain
  To kiss her golden hair, and maidens gay.

June brought her roses, crimson, pink and white,
  And blue forget-me-nots, and foxgloves tall,
With sweet carnations and delphiniums bright,
  And flowers from field and hedge, both great and small.

And when she saw them with'ring one by one,
  Her blue eyes filled with tears, that fell on them,
And made them bloom anew, kissed by the sun,
  Which made each teardrop sparkle like a gem.

Then as June slipped away, forth July came,
  Her arms were full of lilies and sweet peas,
With masses of nasturtiums red as flame,
  And honeysuckle, loved by all the bees.

Lastly came August, bringing poppies red,
  Bright golden sunflowers, sweet harebells that peep
From out the grass. Then Summer drooped her head
  Saying 'I am weary now, and I will sleep.'

She sank to rest upon a bed of flowers,
  And August bore her in her arms away
To rest a year among far distant bowers,
  While o'er the land rich Autumn held her sway.

OLIVE MARY VENNER (1910).

Epitaph in Borley Churchyard.

HERE in this tomb's sepulchral shade,
Lo! Edward Waldegrave is laid;
And Frances, too, now life is sped,
Here shares his tomb, as once his bed.
The wife with food the poor supplied,
In prison bonds the husband died,
Their progeny, in strength and grace,
Increased the honours of the race.
What profit, man, when life is cold,
In titles, pedigree, or gold?
The frame dissolved, nought meets thy sight;
Earth claims her own, the stars their right.

Translated by GEORGE COURTAULD.

To a Roast Pig

O PIG, or rather, little pork, once pig,
Smoking so daintily upon the table,
Making each gazer long that he were able,
To eat thee every limb, both small and big,
No more in squeaking flight, or grunting jig,
Thou runn'st about the straw-yard, stye, or stable,
Nor bump'st thy little side against the gable ;
Nor cock'st thy snout, a judge without a wig !
All other viands which I ever saw
Served up in silver, crockery ware, or tin,
Whether boil'd, roasted, bak'd, stew'd, fried or raw,
Compar'd with thee are worthless as a pin !
Sweet delicate meat ! crackling without a flaw !
What ho ! a knife and fork ! I must begin !

C. LESINGHAM SMITH, *Footprints, &c.* 1868.

Acorning

RIPE on the oaks are the acorns, prowling abroad is the small boy,
Watch him carefully, thou, lest he may do thee an ill ;
Not that thou grudgest the fruit beloved of the good piggy-wiggy,
But on the small boy's steps mischief is wont to attend ;
Trampling gaps in the hedges, damaging fences in climbing,
Flinging open the gates, tempting the cattle to stray ;
Wrenching boughs from the saplings, gathering stones from the wayside,
Shying them into the trees, careless on whom they may fall.

Cheekily answering back, remonstrance lightly regarding,
Or, if business is meant, speedily scudding away;
If on pursuit thou determine, and if thou succeed in his capture,
Rises the difficult point—what's to be done with him then?
Shall he be haled to the judgment in charge of the man in blue raiment,
Where, for the children's fault, parents their purses must open?
Nay, let his father reprove him, his mother with timeous spankings
Give him a lesson at home, teaching him how to behave.

GEORGE COURTAULD, *Rhymes Old and New*, 1910.

King Cole of Colchester

NOW, lords and ladies, leave, I pray,
For a song to pass the time away;
I will sing of a King who was good and gay,
And great in ancient story:
He reigned in a town which all men know,
Where the cornfields wave, and the roses blow,
And the dainty, delicate oysters grow,
To add to its fame and glory.

Chorus—

Old King Cole,
Rest his jolly soul!
And may we all live like him in content and harmony.
So keep the music going,
And the bowl of friendship flowing,
And the happy roses growing
Over England fair and free!

Now Old King Cole was not strait-laced;
He was fifty inches round the waist;

And he wasn't exactly pasty-faced,
        For he liked the flowing bowl, oh!
His heart was warm, and his hand was free,
He loved good cheer and company,
And the twang, twang, twang of his fiddlers three;
        Then hey for Old King Cole, oh!
    Chorus—Old King Cole, etc.

King Cole was a minstrel good and true;
His merry pipe went tootle-too,
And he played in tune as a King should do,
        And his people loved to hear him.
He justice did in every case,
And whatsoe'er the time or place,
He never turned his jolly face
        From the poor folk crowding near him.
    Chorus—Old King Cole, etc.

But the Roman hosts came swarming down
On Colchester, that famous town,
And Old King Cole would have lost his crown
        If it had not been for his daughter;
For Helena, who was fair as day,
She met Constantius on the way,
And she said, 'Please put that sword away,
        And let's have no more slaughter!'
    Chorus—Old King Cole, etc.

Constantius was a man of might,
But he fell in love at very first sight,
And he said, 'Young woman, I'm done for quite!'
        So woe was turned to laughter:
For of course she didn't know what to say,
And of course she blushed and turned away,
And the fiddlers played on the wedding day,
        And they all lived happy after.
    Chorus—Old King Cole, etc.

W. Gurney Benham. (1909).

The Song of the Spade

O, I AM the first of the whole world's tools,
For I came when the world began ;
And my primitive form has withstood the storm
Of that change which has touched even man ;
The eldest and humblest, the first and last,
Poor aristocrat of the soil ;
With a pedigree longer than kings can boast—
And the end of all human toil.

I call to you, call to you : Leave your books,
And come back to the primal source ;
With arms bared and brown, now so whitened in town,
I will make you a man of force.
And I call to the trader, the artizan,
To the clerk and the workshop 'hand,'
Give a space of your time, for your body and soul,
To your patches of household land.

O, I sing not a song of the workshop dense,
With its foul and stagnant air ;
But I chant you a strain of sweet herb and grain,
Of the bloom that is soft and fair.
I bring you no pallid or sunken cheeks,
Nor a cough and a premature death :
I give you the strength and the glorious wealth
That come on the fresh wind's breath.

Then, here's to the heart that delights in me,
To the hand with the grip of man ;
To the honest thought, not of custom wrought
That this life is a trading span.
I call to you : Come to the cool brown earth,
To the work that is health and gain,
To the scent of soil that is worth your moil—
To a pleasure that brings no pain.

O, a million healths and a thousand wealths,
 And the wide earth spread at his feet,
To the man who finds, as through life he winds,
 That my haft to his hand is sweet.
For the man who can say in his inmost heart,
 As he delves in the cool moist earth,
That my handle he loves, as a woman loves,
 Has a treasure that's greater than birth.

J. E. Patterson, *Tillers of the Soil*, 1911.

PROVERBS, EPIGRAMS, AND BELL MOTTOES

WHEN the wind's in the East, it's neither good for man nor beast.

As the days lengthen, so the cold strengthens.

HE that would live for aye must eat sage in May.

ESSEX stiles, Kentish miles, Norfolk wiles, many men beguiles.

MEAT is much, but manners is more.

MUCH water goes by the mill the miller knows not of.

HIS cockloft is unfurnished.

JOHN RAY.

ESSEX, you say, is famed for Calves;
We thank you really for your pains,
For thus you prove in our behalves
We're famous most for *Head* and *Brains*.

G. T. MANNING.

Proverbs

WHO goeth a borrowing
Goeth a sorrowing
Few lend (but fools)
Their working tools.

WHAT greater crime
Than loss of time.

FEBRUARY, fill the dyke
With that thou dost like.

MARCH dust to be sold
Worth ransom of gold.

PAY justly thy tithes, whatsoever they be,
That God may in blessing send foison to thee;
Though Vicar be bad, or the Parson as evil,
Go not for thy tithing thyself to the Devil.

WHAT better fare than well content?

POSIES FOR THINE OWN BEDCHAMBER

What better bed than conscience good, to pass the night with sleep?
What better work than daily care fro' sin thyself to keep?
What better thought than think on God, and daily him to serve?
What better gift than to the poor that ready be to sterve?

THOMAS TUSSER,
Five Hundred Points of Good Husbandry.

WHEN the Fern is as high as a spoon
You may sleep an hour at noon.
When the Fern is as high as a ladle,
You may sleep as long as you are able;
When the Fern begins to look red
Then milk is good with brown bread.

IF Candlemas Day be fair and bright
Winter will have another flight:
If on Candlemas Day it be shower and rain,
Winter is gone and will not come again.

THE love of a woman and a bottle of wine,
Are sweet for a season, but last for a time.

PENNY and penny laid up will be many,
Who will not keep a penny shall never have many.

GOOD riding at two Anchors men have told,
For if one break, 'tother may hold.

THE higher the plum tree, the riper the plum,
The richer the cobbler, the blacker his thumb.

A MAN of words and not of deeds,
Is like a garden full of weeds.

OUR fathers which were wondrous wise,
Did wash their throats, before they wash't their
eyes.

CHILDREN pick up words as pigeons pease,
And utter them again as God shall please.

THERE or thereabouts, as Parson Smith says.
(Proverbial about Dunmow in Essex.)

BRAINTREE for the pure,
Bocking for the poor,
Cogshall for the jeering town, and
Kelvedon for the boor.

WITH a red man reade thy read;
With a brown man break thy bread:
At a pale man draw thy knife:
From a black man keep thy wife.

JOHN RAY, *English Proverbs*, 1670.

The devil was sick, the devil a monk would be,
The devil was well, the devil a monk was he.

Make haste when you are purchasing a field, but when you are to marry a wife, be slow.

If I had not lifted up the stone, you had not found the jewel.

Richard Kidder, *Hebrew Proverbs*, 1737.

Let every house sweep the dirt from its own doorstep, and then the whole street will soon bee clean. For there bee those that weare the Lord's Livery, and doe the Devil's work all the day long.

Stephen Marshall, *Sermon.*

The Months

January

Roast Beef, Strong Ale, Good Fires, are now
three things
Which this cold Season much contentment brings.

February

The Four and twentieth day the Stars fore-tell,
Of Pancakes and of Fritters a great smell;
And many hundred Cocks their death shall meet
By Boys throwing Cudgels at them in the street.

March

Now doth the Spring put on her new Apparel,
And the kind Butler broaches a fresh barrel;
The days and nights are even without a quarrel,
When Summercomes, Winter must take its farewell.

April

Now Lasses into Groves and Meadows gets,
To gather Primroses and Violets;
But let them heed they do not too far stray,
Lest they their Maiden-heads do lose that way.

JUNE

Now Phœbus he his greatest strength forth yields,
And Beggars scorn the Barns, and lie in Fields;
If laziness do in some people lurk,
A whip laid on their backs will make them work.

AUGUST

Now Virgo rules, the Maid by whom is born,
In her fair hands the ripened ears of Corn.

SEPTEMBER

This month having an R. in't, is the reason,
That Oysters they do come again in season.

OCTOBER

Fair Summer's Pride begins to fade away,
And night t' encroach upon the hours of day;
The winged Choristers do cease their notes,
And stately Forests don their yellow coats.

DECEMBER

Now stormy blasts enforce the quaking trees,
To wrap their trembling Limbs in mossy freize,
Roast Beef, minc'd Pies, are good to those that try them,
But the worst of it is how to come by them.

HENRY WINSTANLEY,
Poor Robin's Almanack, 1691.

So many dayes old the moon is on Michaelmas day, so many Floods will be that winter.

Ibid.

CHELMSFORD Church, and Writtle steeple,
Both fell down, but killed no people.

He who cures a disease may be the skilfulest, but he that prevents it is the safest Physician.

Men have a touchstone whereby to try gold ;
But gold is a touchstone whereby to try men.

He lives long that lives well.

Thomas Fuller.

Our God and Soldier we alike adore,
When at the brink of ruin, not before ;
After deliverance both alike requited,
Our God forgotten, and our soldiers slighted.

Quarles.

High God! What a sweet thing is Danger past.

William Bedell.

On William Gilbert, M.D., friend and favourite physician of Queen Elizabeth, the illustrious pioneer of electrical science, born at Colchester, 1540.

Among the asserters of free reason's claim,
Our nation's not the least in worth or fame,
The world to Bacon does not only owe
Its present knowledge, but its future too.
Gilbert shall live, till loadstones cease to draw,
Or British fleets the boundless ocean awe.

John Dryden, *To Dr. Charleton.*

I have observed that many old proverbs are very true, and amongst the rest, this: 'It is better to be at the latter end of a feast than at the beginning of a fray,' for most commonly, those that are in the beginning of a fray get but little of the feast, and those that have undergone the greatest dangers have least of the spoils.

Margaret, Duchess of Newcastle, 1667.

WHENEVER God erects a house of prayer
The Devil always builds a chapel there,
And 'twill be found upon examination
The latter has the largest congregation.

DANIEL DEFOE,
The True-born Englishman, 1701.

THOUGH man a thinking being is defined
Few use the great prerogative of mind,
How few think justly of the thinking few !
How many never think who think they do.

JANE TAYLOR.

SALUTE and be saluted.

PERFECT men and perfect horses nobody ever sees.

USE what you have that you may have more to use.

RELATIVES are best with a wall between them.

GOD'S providence is mine inheritance.

EVERY man is a volume if you know how to read him.

ONE must plough with the horses one has.

No sense so uncommon as common sense.

C. H. SPURGEON, *The Salt-Cellars*, 1889.

Do not be all sugar, or the world will suck you down ; but do not be all vinegar, or the world will spit you out.

SORROWS are visitors that come without invitation, but complaining minds send a waggon to bring their troubles home in.

SPENDING your money with many a guest,
Empties the larder, the cellar and chest.

CARVE your name on hearts and not on marble.

C. H. SPURGEON,
John Ploughman's Talk, 1868.

A Clerical Humourist

Epigrams

SOME one having said of Macaulay, 'He will let nobody talk but himself,' Sidney Smith at once answered, 'Why, who would if he could help it?'

Mrs. B. has not very clear ideas about the tides. I remember, at a large party, her insisting that it was always high tide at London Bridge at twelve o'clock. She referred to me.

'Now, Mr. Smith, is it not so?'

I answered, 'It used not to be so, I believe, formerly, but perhaps the Lord Mayor and Aldermen have altered it lately.'

No, I don't like dogs; I always expect them to go mad. A lady asked me once for a motto for her dog Spot. I proposed, 'Out, damned Spot,' but she did not think it sentimental enough.

Marriage resembles a pair of shears, so joined that they cannot be separated; often moving in opposite directions, yet always punishing any one who comes between them.

There are many people who run about after happiness like an absent-minded man hunting for his hat, which all the while is on his head.

What a pity it is that in England we have no amusements but vice and religion.

In the country! Oh, in the country I always fear that creation will expire before tea-time.

Country life is very good, in fact, the best—for cattle.

What a beautiful thought—a sunbeam passes through pollution unpolluted.

SYDNEY SMITH, *Wit and Wisdom*, 1860.

Colchester Town Hall

Bell Mottoes LINES inscribed on the five bells hung under the crown forming apex of belfry; specially composed.

I

Placed here on high,
We serve the town,
Beneath the crown,
Beneath the sky.

II

Differing in size,
In note and weight,
Yet, small or great,
We harmonise.

III

With measured speech,
Well-timed and true,
Our message due
We tell to each.

IV

Brief, clear and bold,
We say our say,
And then straightway
Our peace we hold.

V

O mortal race,
Our lesson learn
Each has his turn,
And time, and place.

W. GURNEY BENHAM, 1899.

Latton Church Bells

At evening hour, yon holy tower
Pours sweetly forth, o'er dale and bower,
Its soothing chimes, like ancient rhymes,—
Forgotten strains of olden times,—
And seems some hoary sage, who tells
A bygone tale by those sweet bells.

But though no more his words have power
To move the heart as once of yore ;
Yet still I feel them o'er me steal,
And faintly to the ear reveal,
That as they mark each closing day,
So, too, they tell, life hastes away.

G. T. Manning, *Essex Literary Journal.*

Great Baddow

1. I mean to make it understood that tho' I'm little yet I'm good.

8. The Founder he hath play'd his part. That shewes he's master of his art. So hang me well, & Ring me true, & I will sound your praises due. Chapman & Mears, Fecerunt 1789.

Sible Hedingham

When yow heare this then doe vs blese.
(Followed by six initials of donors).

Chelmsford : St. Mary

To honour both of God and King
Our voices shall in consort ring.

Hornchurch: St. Andrew

Bell Mottoes 3. If you have a judicious ear
you 'll own my voice is sweet and clear.
5. Ye ringers all that prize your health & happiness be sober,
merry wise & you will the same possess.
6. Ye people all that hear me ring
Be faithful to your God and King.

In the Ringing Chamber there was also formerly a set of old ringing rules (now superseded by a prosaic modern set) which ran:—

If you ring with Spur or Hat
Three pints of beer you pay For that
If you swear or give the Lye
A pot you pay Immediately.
If a bell you overthrow
A pint you pay before you go.

Maldon: All Saints

1. When three this steeple long did hold
2. They ware three emblems of a scold
3. No musick then But now shall see
4. What pleasant musick six will be.—1707.

High Ongar

Whilst thus we join in chearful sound, May love and loyalty abound.—1775.

Prittlewell

1. A royal Peal are we
To ring o'er land and sea
From Prittlewell Belfry.—1902.
4. When sweetly sounds this bell
From tower of Prittlewell
Let Jesus Christ be praised.

Springfield

On a tablet in the ringing loft of All Saints, Springfield, is the following: *Bell Mottoes*

If that to ring you do come here
You must ring well with hands and ear.
But if you ring in spur or hat,
Fourpence is always due for that.
And if a bell you overthrow,
Sixpence is due before you go.
But if you either sweare or curse,
Twelvepence is due—out with your purse.
Our laws are old, they are not new
Therefore the Clerk must have his due.
If to our laws you do consent
Then take a bell, we are content.

Upminster

3. God Save our Nobel Qveene Elisabeth.—1602.

Walthamstow: St. Mary

The inscriptions are worth quoting as specimens of the poetical genius which shed its afflatus over their larger rings.

3. All though I am both light and small, I will be heard above you all.
4. Peace and good neighbourhood.
5. At proper times our voices we will raise
In sounding to our benefactors praise.
6. Our voices shall with joyful sound
Make hills and valleys echo round.
7. Whilst thus we join in cheerful sound
May love and loyalty abound.

8. Ye singers all that prize your health and happiness
Be sober, merry, wise and you'll the same possess.
9. In wedlock bands all ye who join with hands your hearts unite
So shall our tunefull tongues combine to laud the nuptial rite.

Wivenhoe

1. May God bless all
Whom we do call.
2. Prosperity
To this church and parish.
3. When sweetly chimes this bell,
O'er sea and hill and dell,
May Jesus Christ be praised.
4. For the honour of God
And the use of this church
These bells were raised.
5. Lord, may this bell for ever be
A tuneful voice o'er land and sea
To call thy people unto thee.
6. This peal of six bells were recast and rehung A.D. 1905, the cost being defrayed by public subscription.

Wormingford

1. Fieri fecerunt venerabilis Gulielmus Waldegrave et Gulielmus Linne generosus 1561.
3. Sit nomen Domini Benedictum.

Cecil Deedes and H. B. Walters.
Church Bells of Essex, 1909.

BIOGRAPHICAL INDEX

Biographical Index.

Printed at
The Westminster Press
411a Harrow Road
London
W